CogAT® Practice Test Level 7 - Questions (Form 7)

Illustrations by: Kenneth Sommer
Written and published by: Bright Kids NYC

Bright Kids NYC Inc.
www.brightkidsnyc.com
info@brightkidsnyc.com
917-539-4575

CogAT® **Practice Test Level 7 - Questions**

Bright Kids NYC

CogAT® Practice Test

Questions

Level 7

Test One:
Picture Analogies

CogAT® **Practice Test Level 7 - Questions**   Bright Kids NYC Inc ©

S1

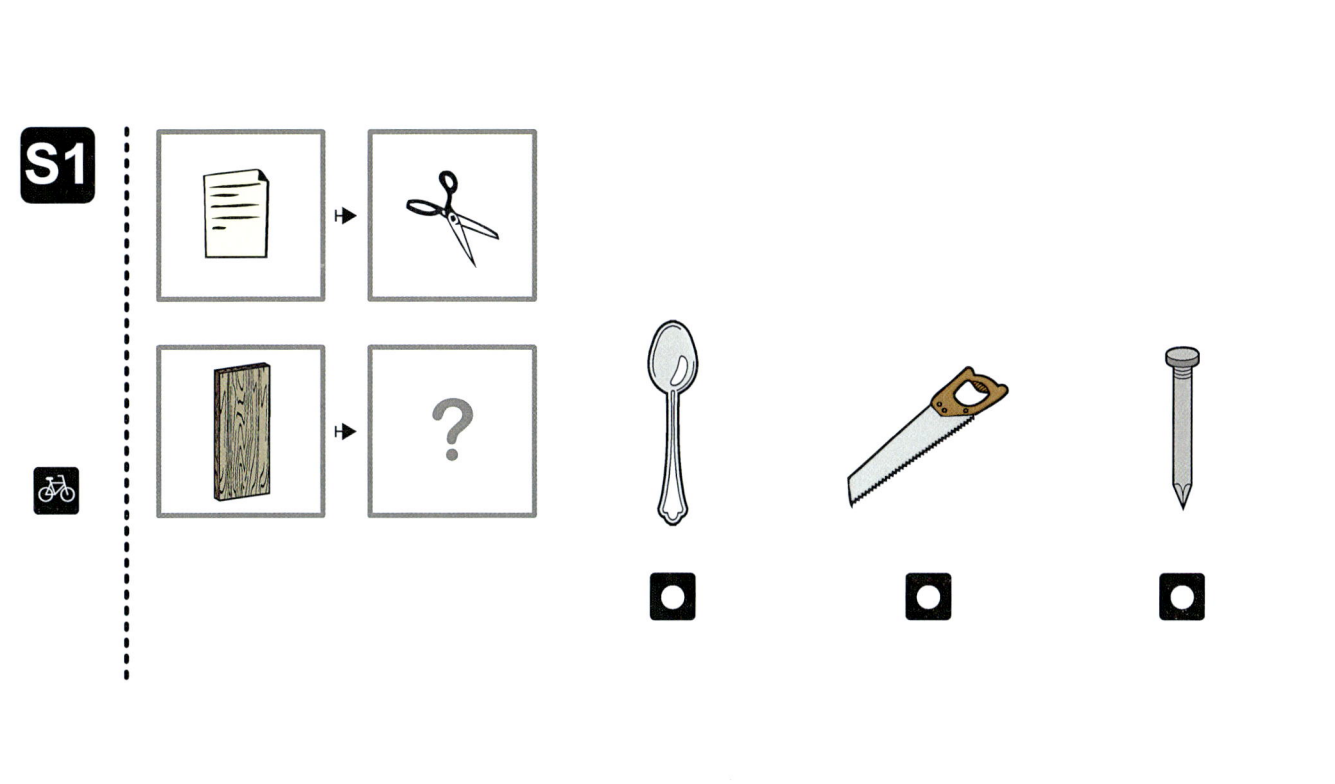

01

02

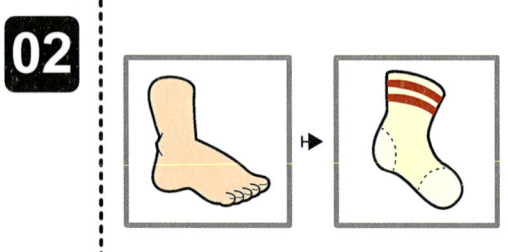

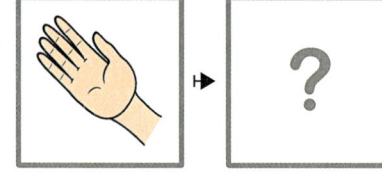  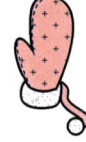

03

04

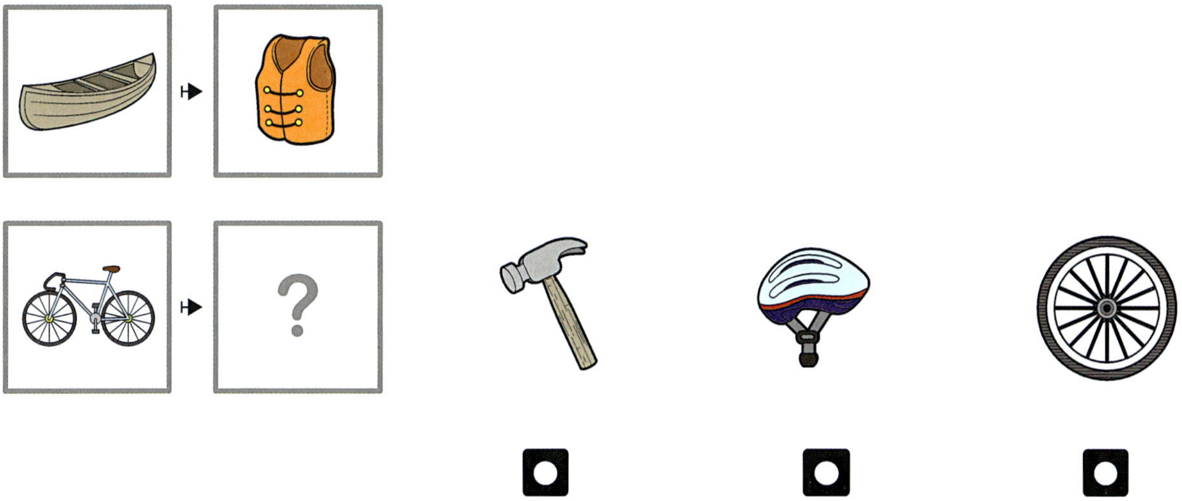

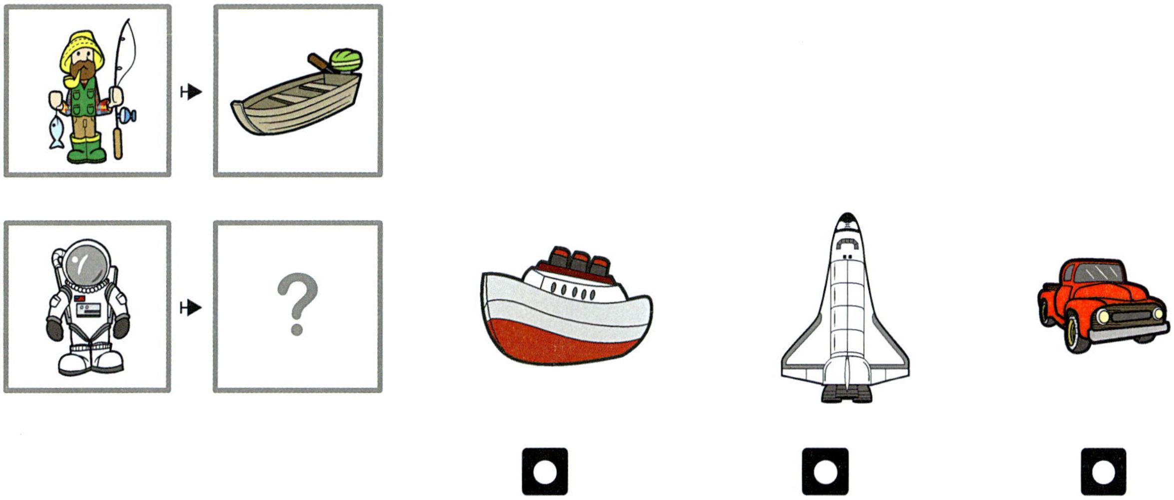

07

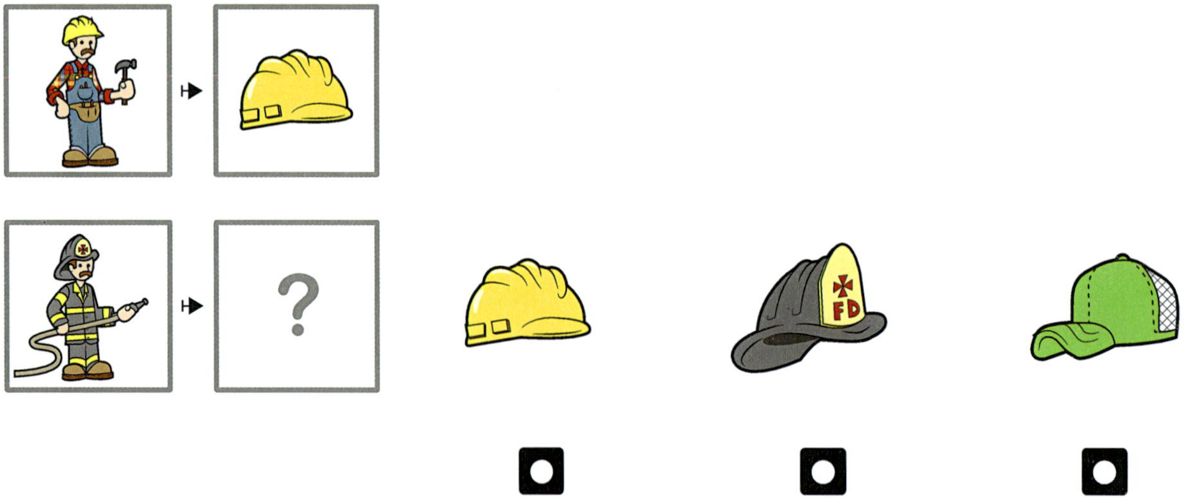

08

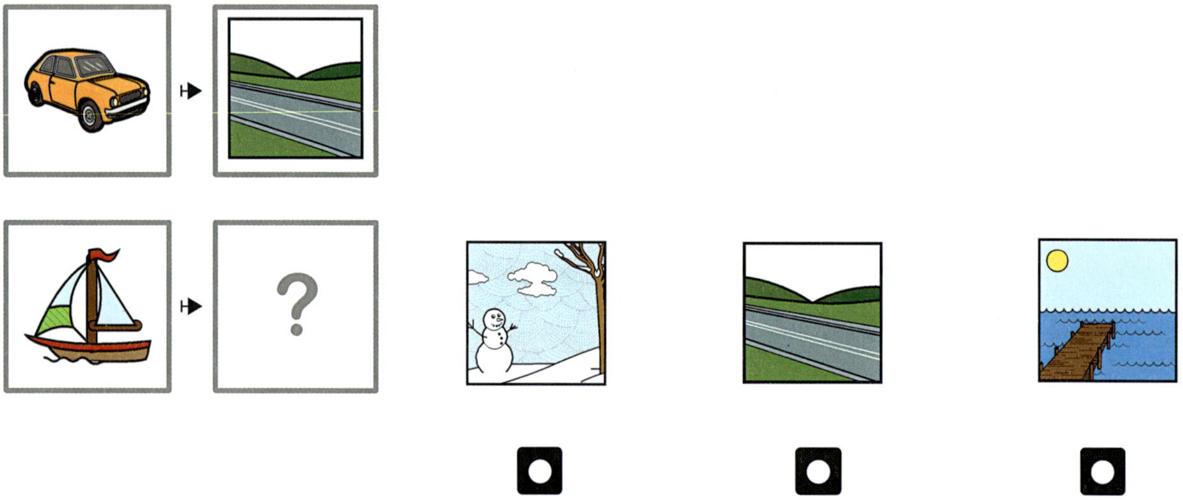

09

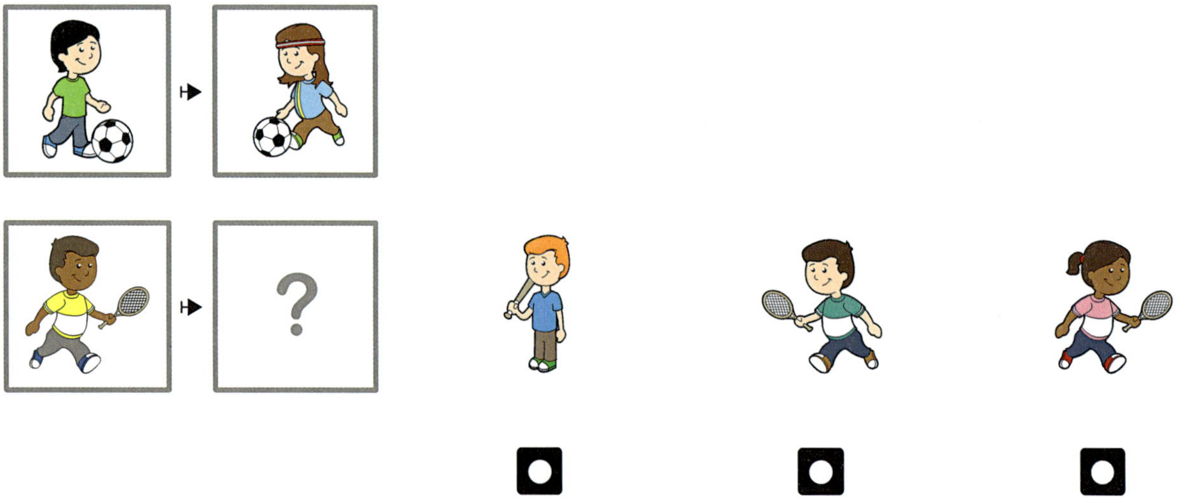

10

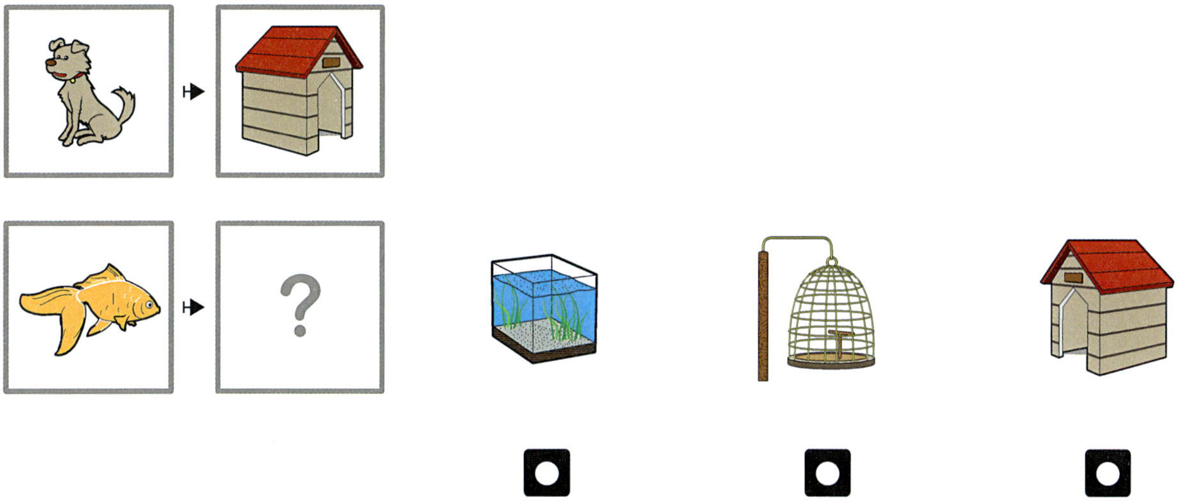

11

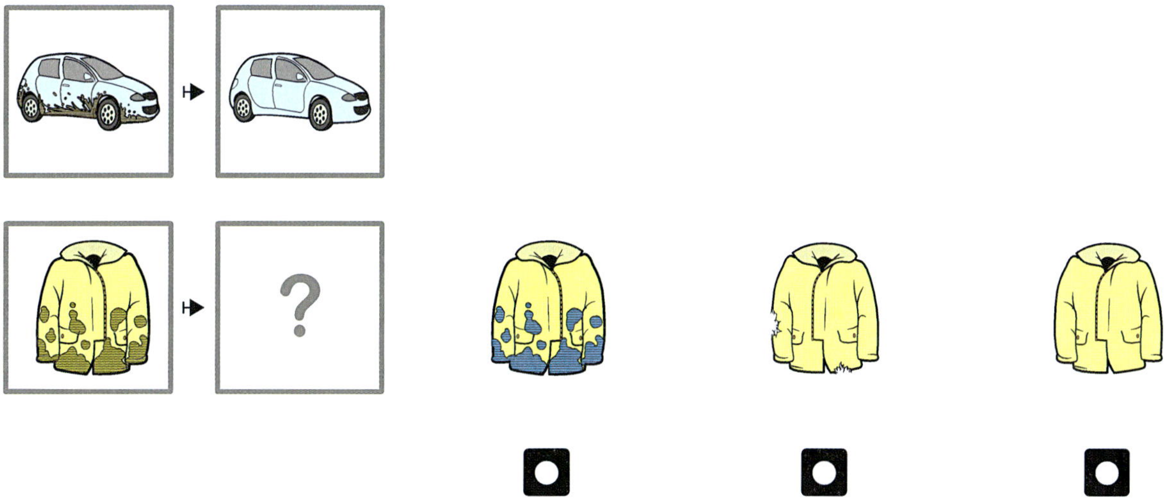

12

13

○   ○   ○

14

○   ○   ○

15

○   ○   ○

16

⭐

CogAT® **Practice Test Level 7 - Questions**   Bright Kids NYC Inc ©

Test Two:
Sentence Completion

CogAT® Practice Test Level 7 - Questions

S1

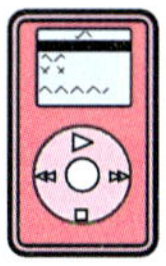

01

   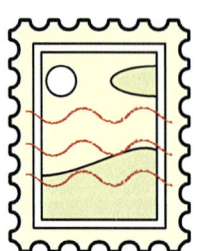   

02

03

04

05

06

07

☀

08

🐚

09

✂

CogAT® Practice Test Level 7 - Questions   Bright Kids NYC Inc ©

10

11

12

13

  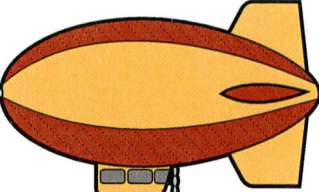

14

15

CogAT® Practice Test Level 7 - Questions   Bright Kids NYC Inc ©

16

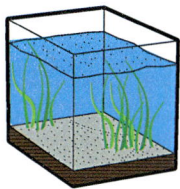      

○   ○   ○

Test Three:
Picture Classification

CogAT® **Practice Test Level 7 - Questions**

S1

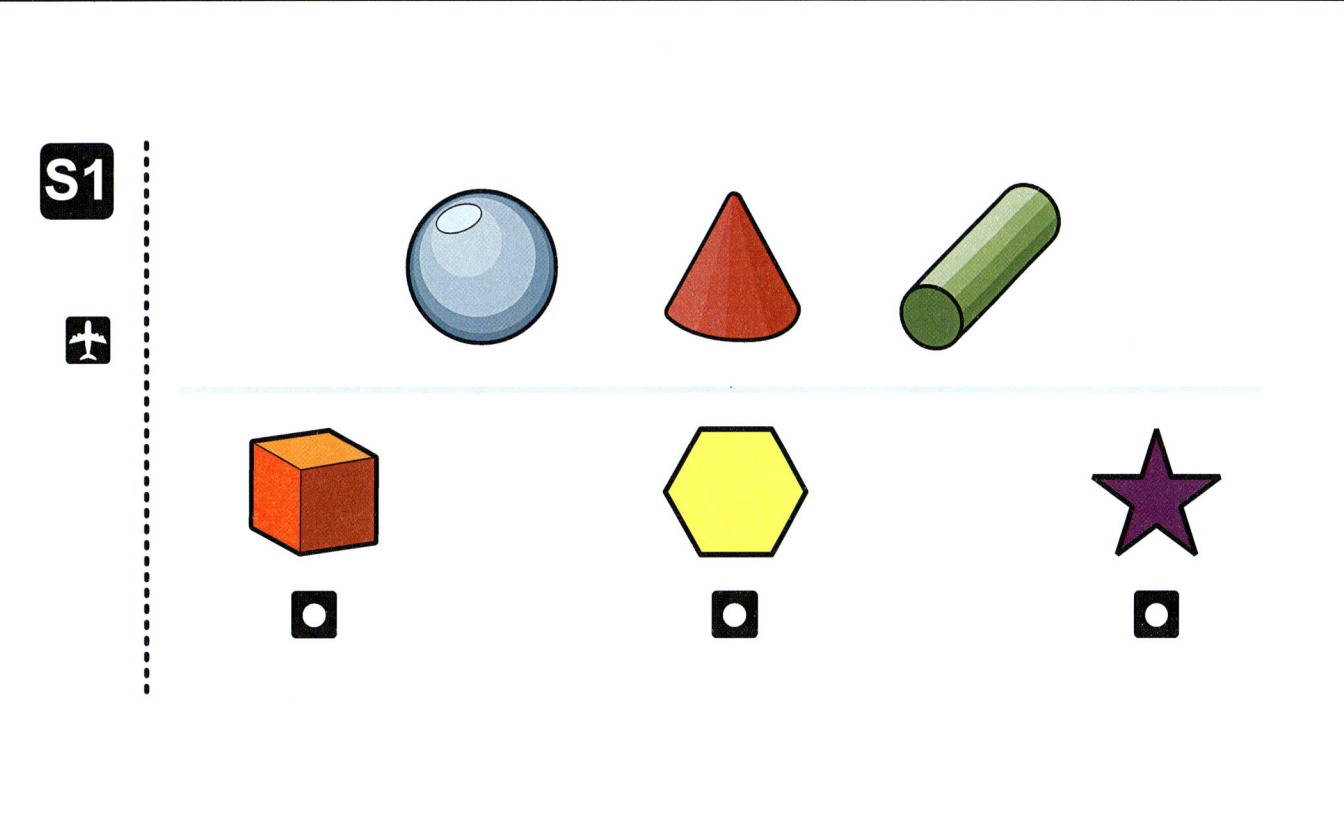

01

02

03

CogAT® Practice Test Level 7 - Questions   Bright Kids NYC Inc ©

04

  ☐

05

  ☐

06

  ☐

07

08

09

CogAT® Practice Test Level 7 - Questions   Bright Kids NYC Inc ©

10

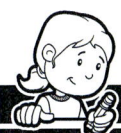

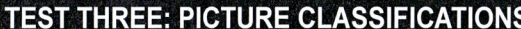

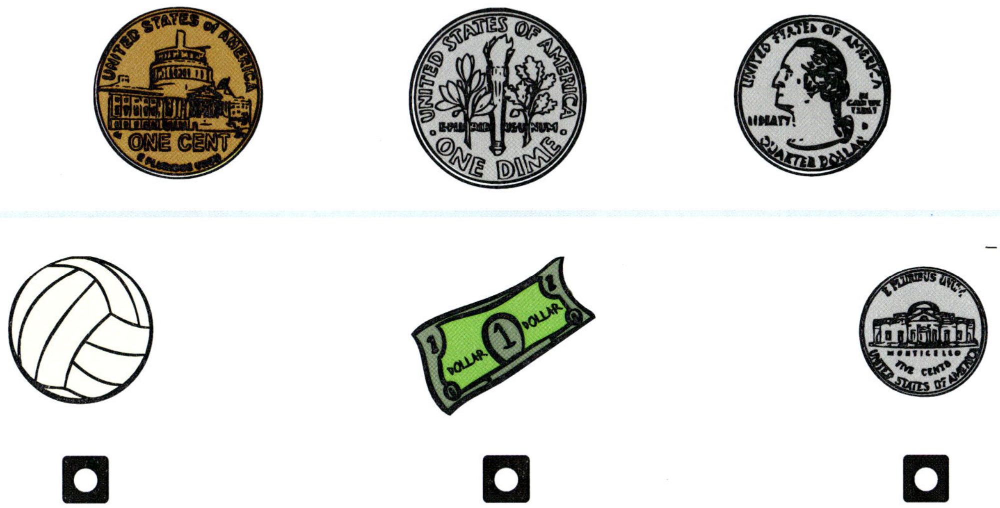
UNITED STATES of AMERICA
ONE CENT
UNITED STATES OF AMERICA
ONE DIME
QUARTER DOLLAR
DOLLAR
FIVE CENTS

11

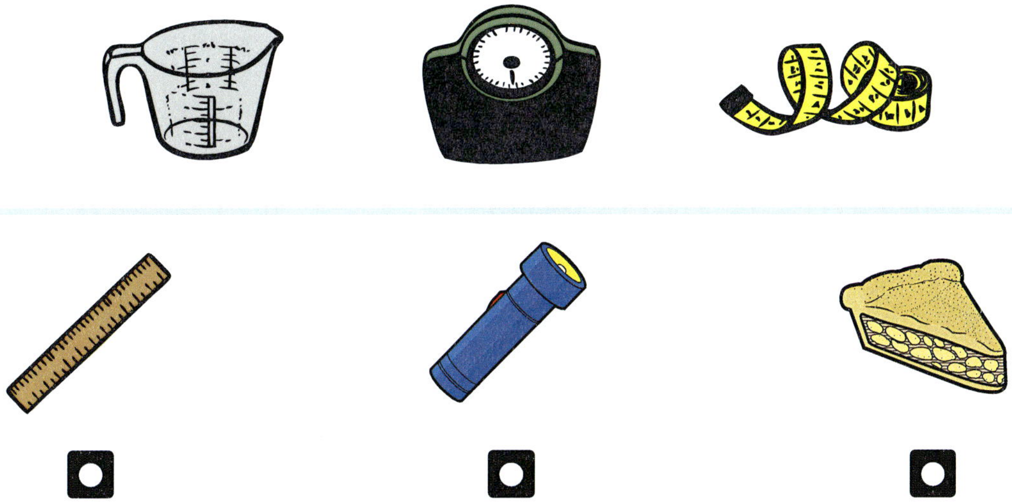

12

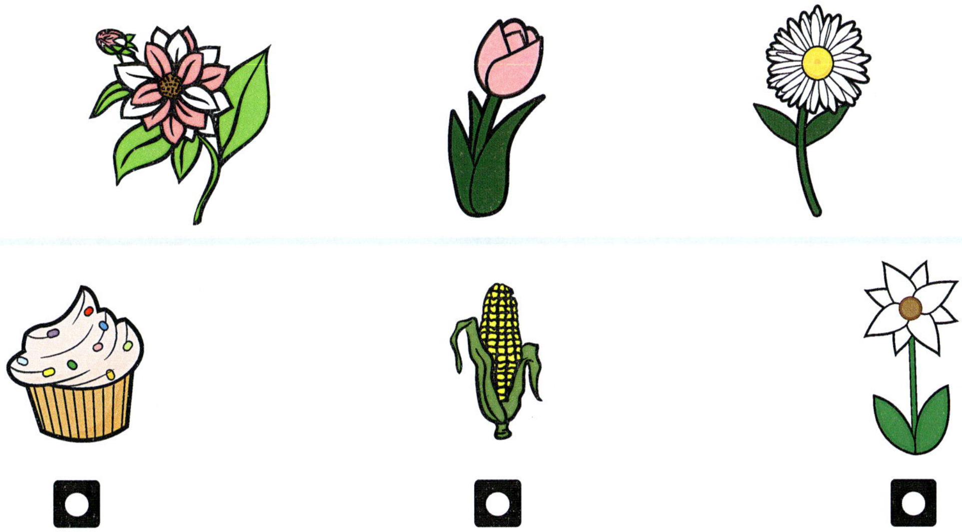

13

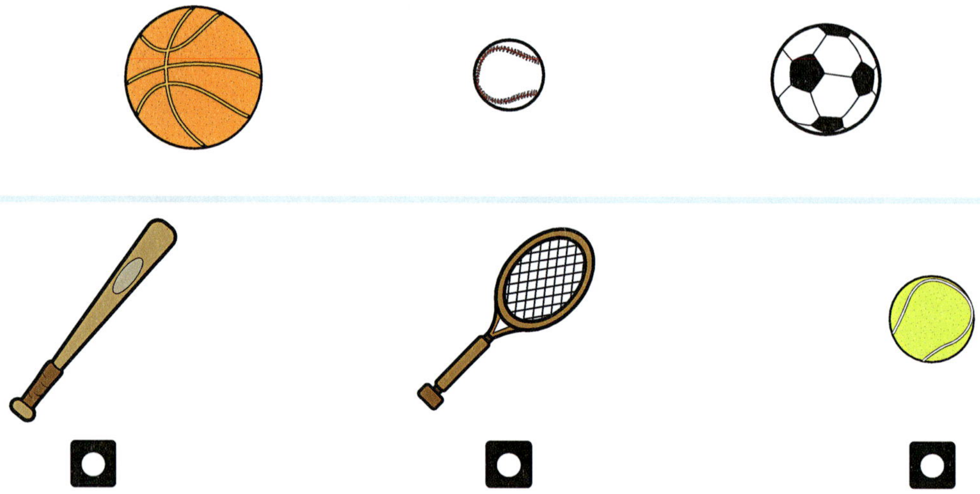

14

15

CogAT® Practice Test Level 7 - Questions   Bright Kids NYC Inc ©

16

  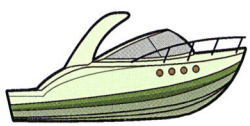

CogAT® **Practice Test Level 7 - Questions**   Bright Kids NYC Inc ©

Test Four:
Number Analogies

CogAT® Practice Test Level 7 - Questions Bright Kids NYC Inc ©

S1

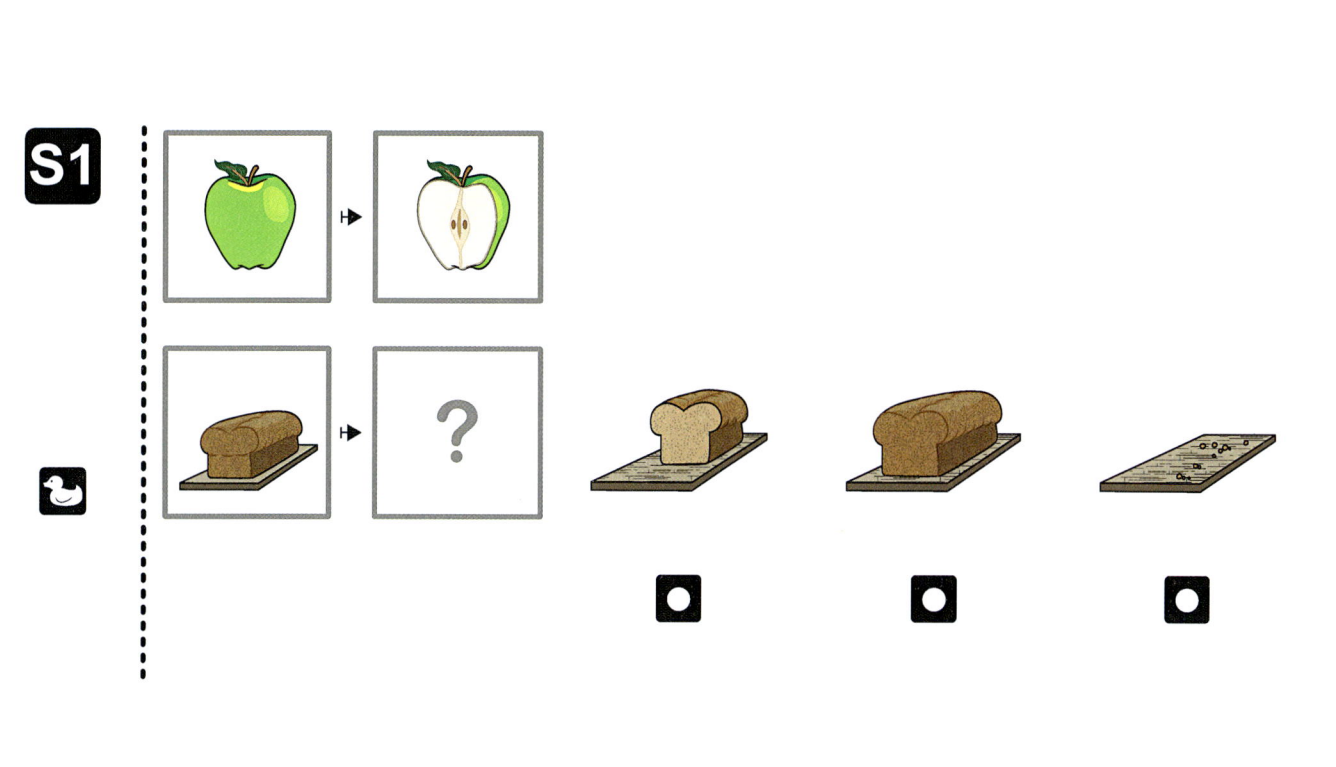

01

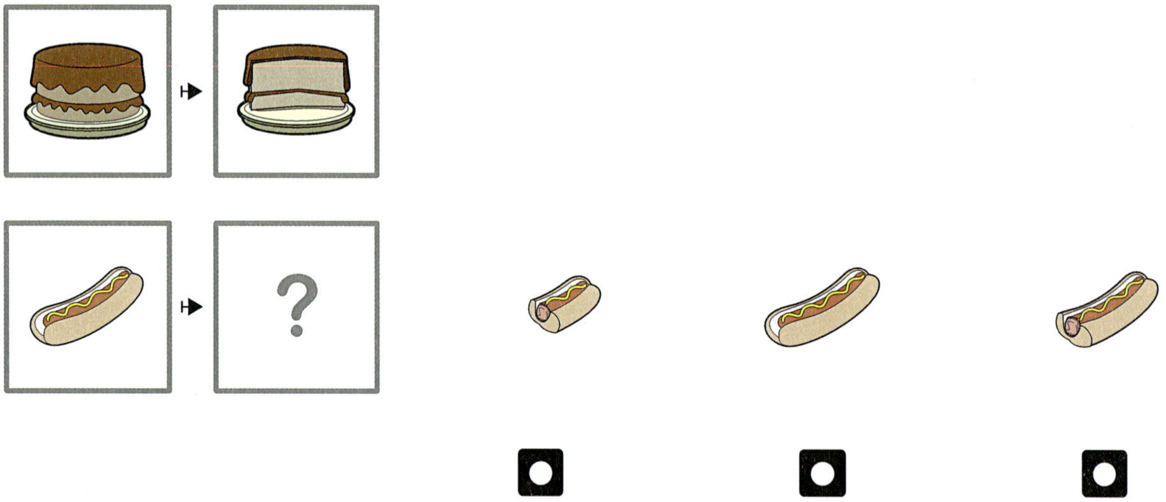

02

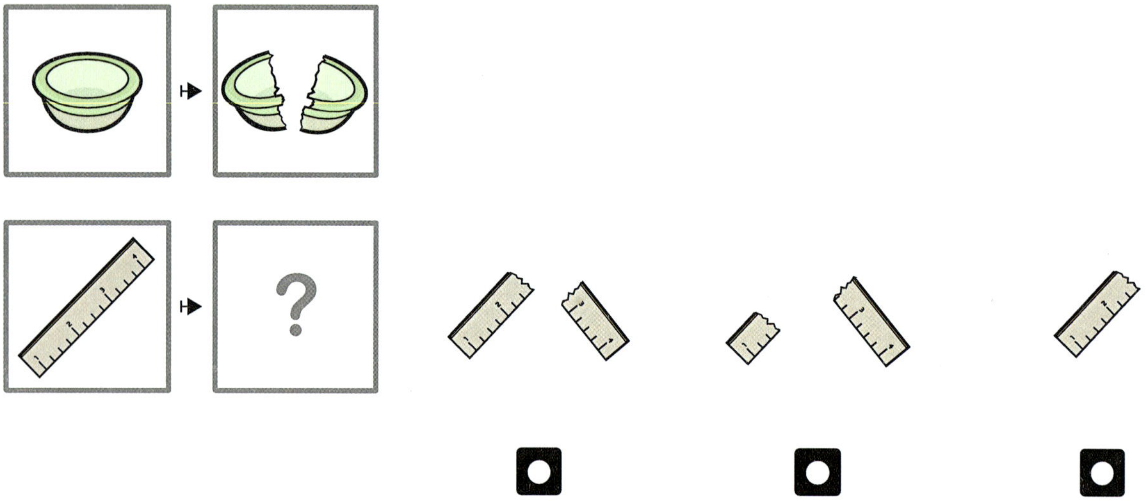

03

CogAT® Practice Test Level 7 - Questions   Bright Kids NYC Inc ©

04

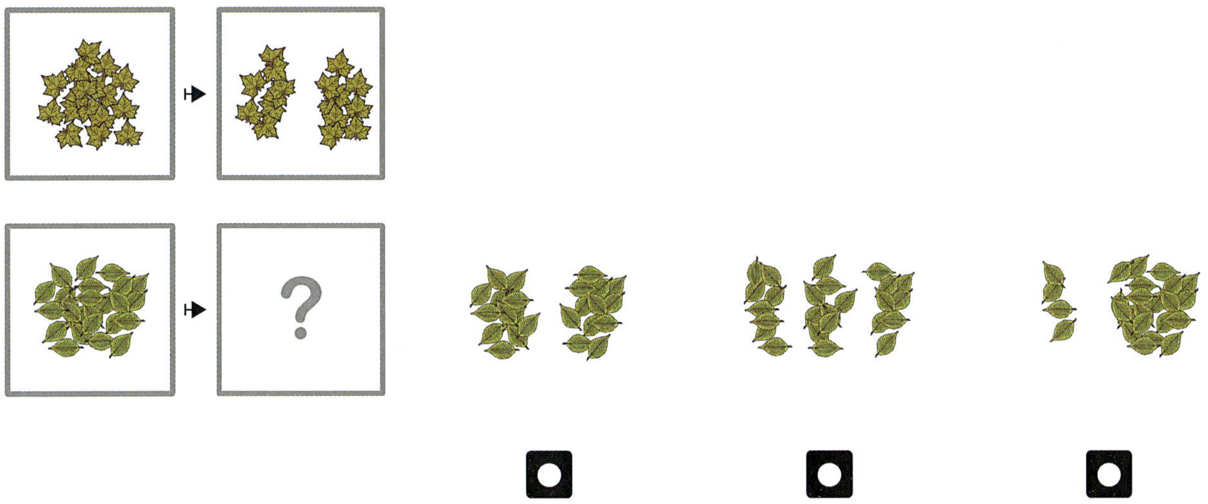

05

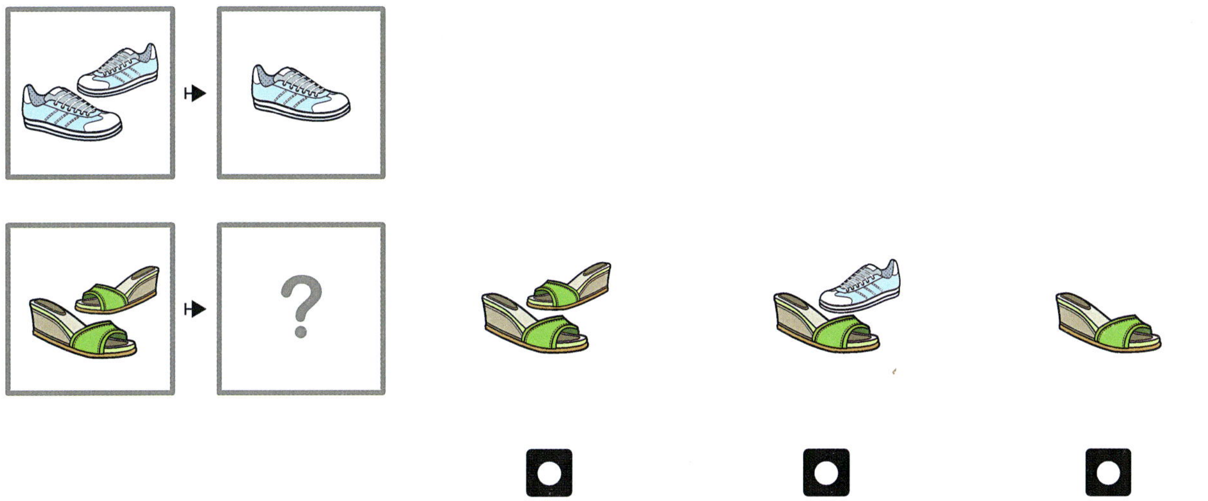

06

07

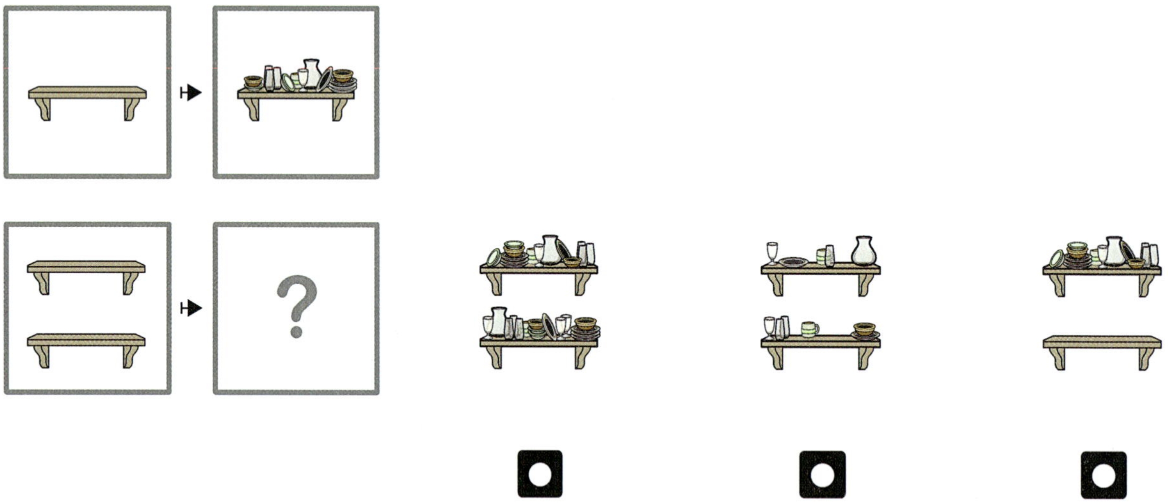

08

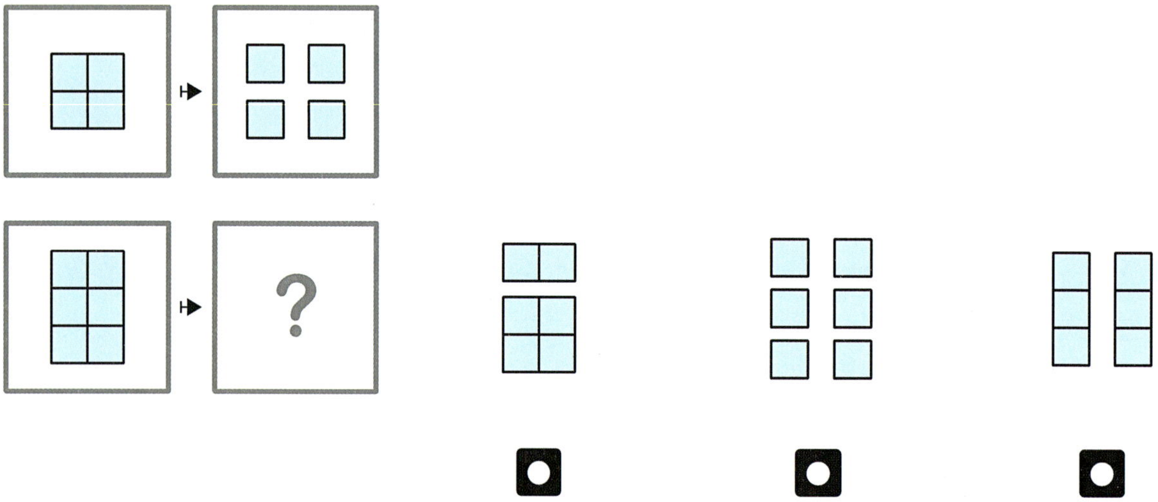

09

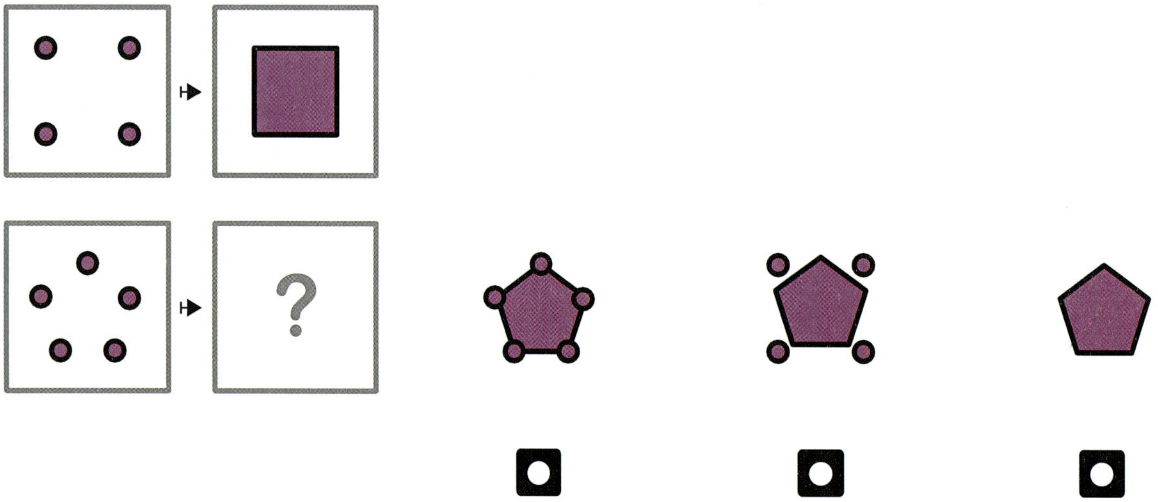

CogAT® Practice Test Level 7 - Questions   Bright Kids NYC Inc ©

10

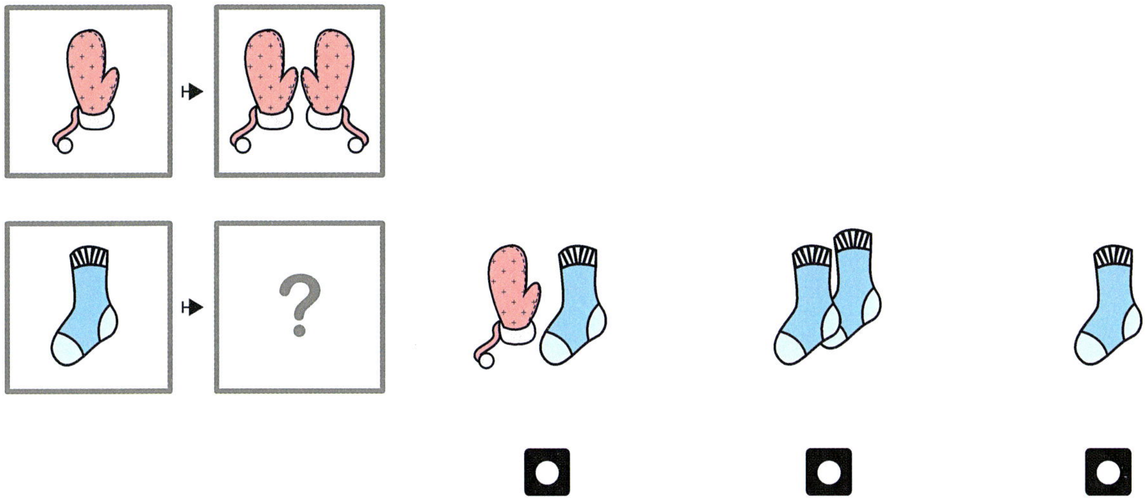

11

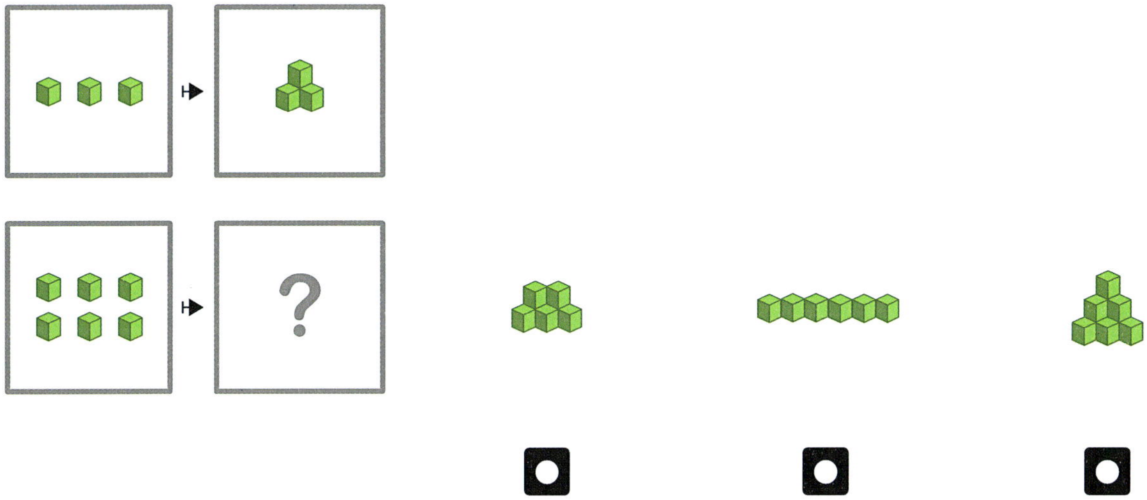

12

13

14

15

16

Test Five:
Number Puzzles

CogAT® **Practice Test Level 7 - Questions**

S1

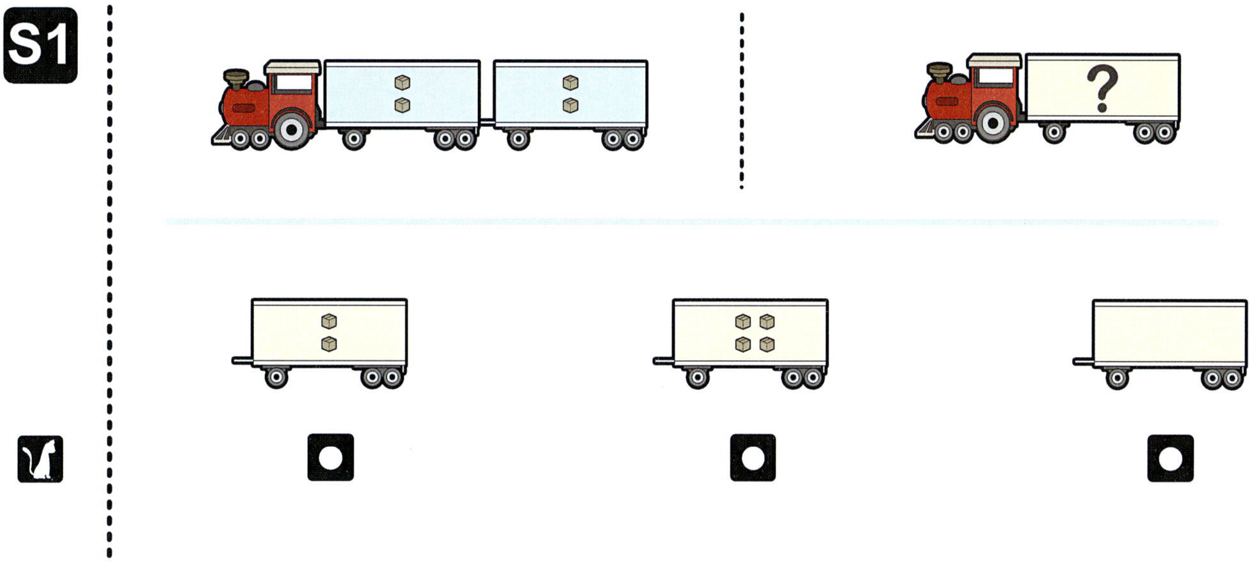

S2

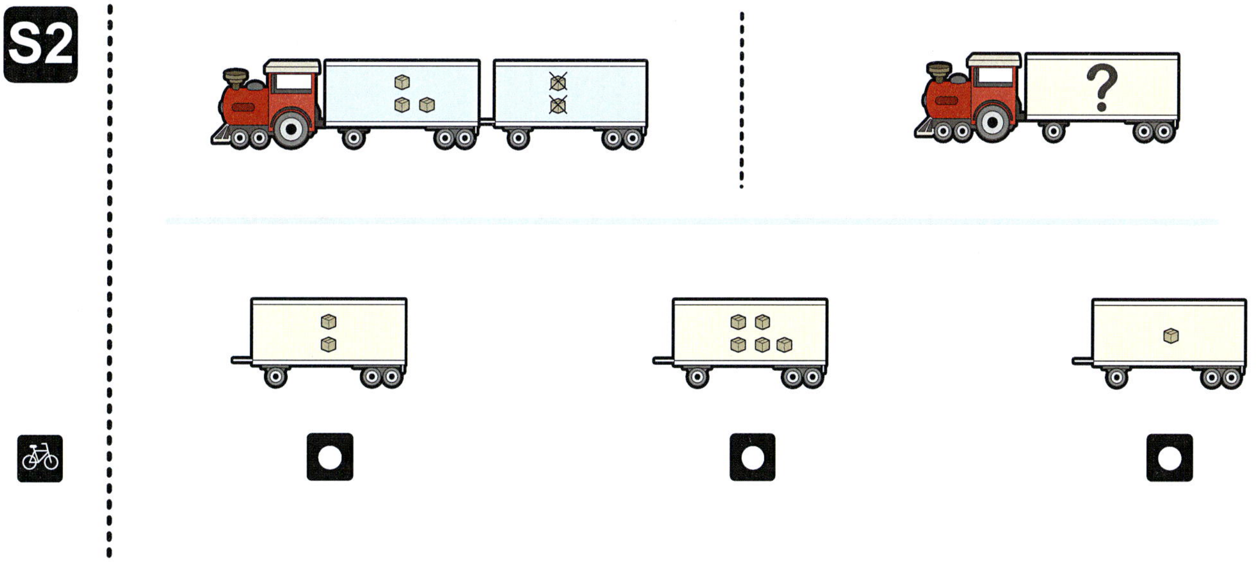

01

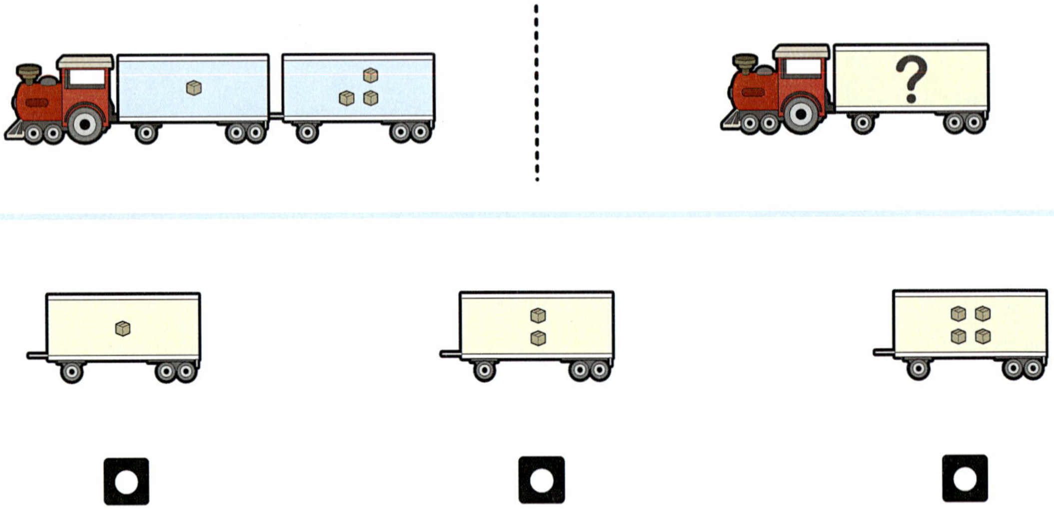

02

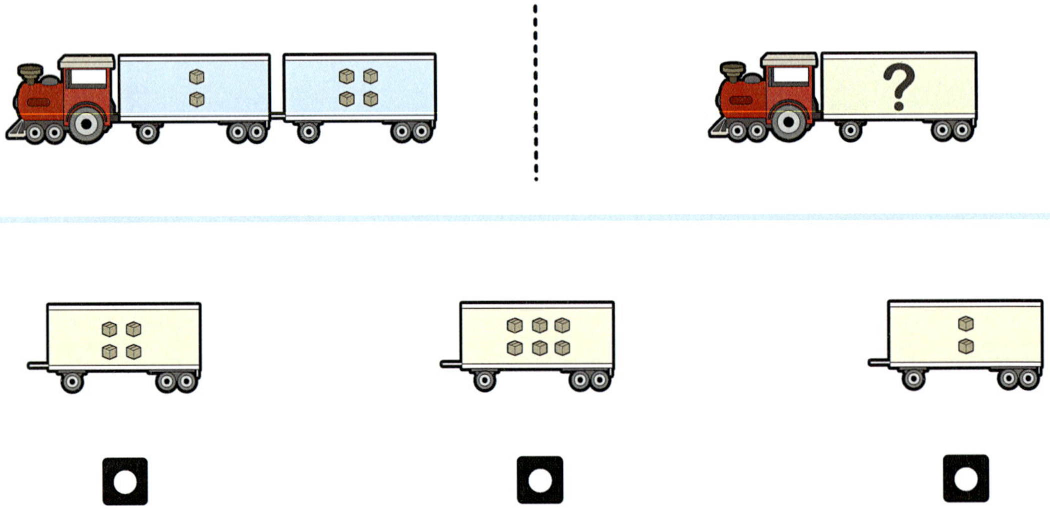

03

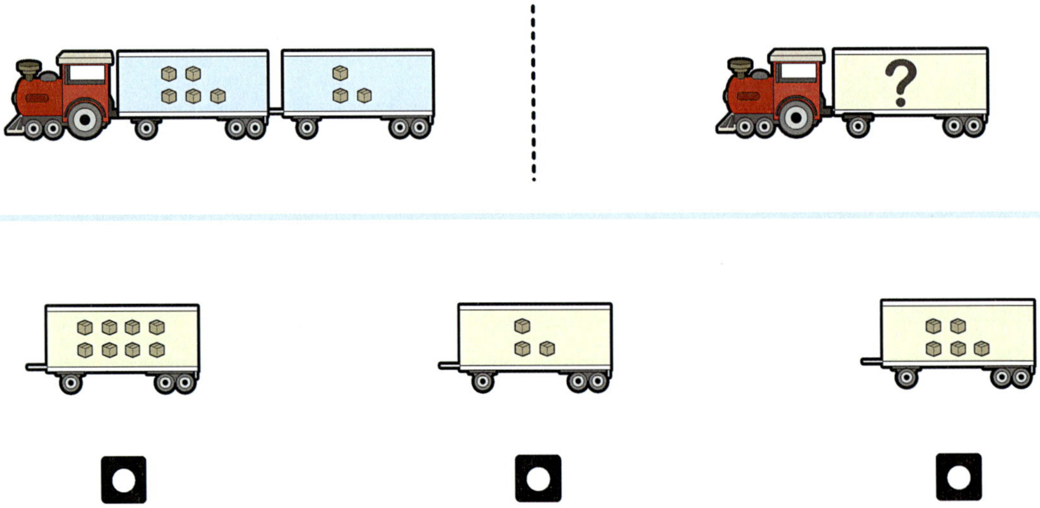

CogAT® Practice Test Level 7 - Questions Bright Kids NYC Inc ©

04

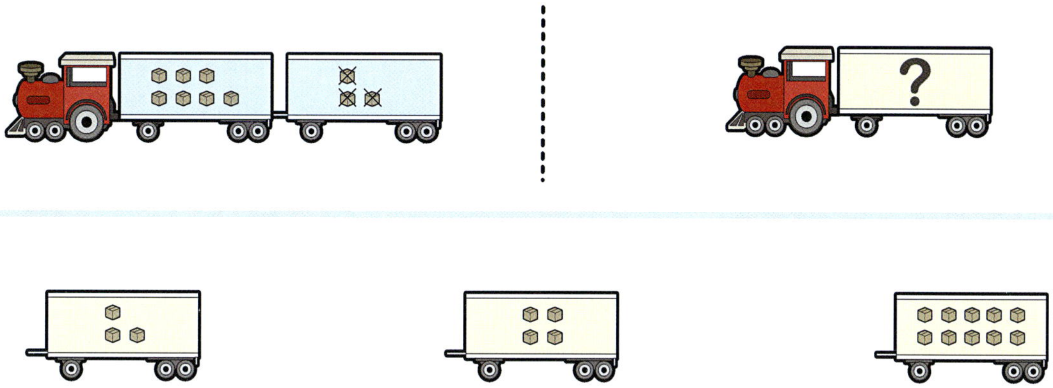

05

06

07

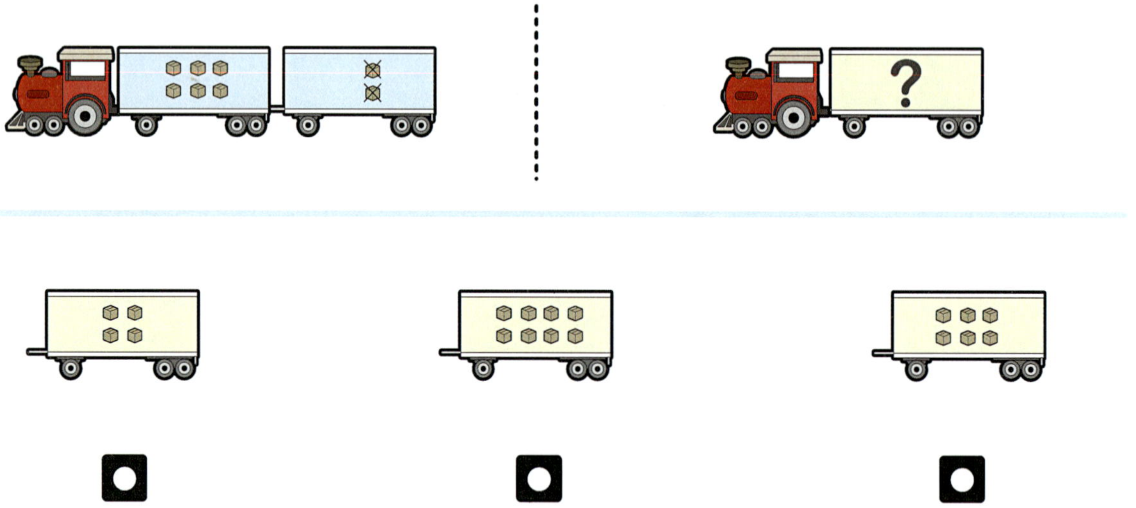

08

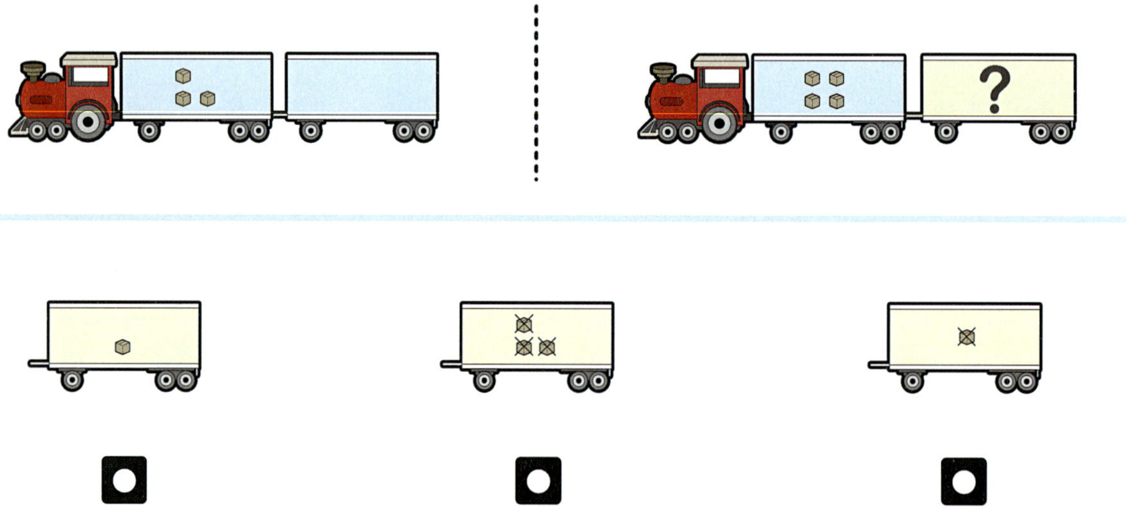

09

CogAT® Practice Test Level 7 - Questions   Bright Kids NYC Inc ©

10

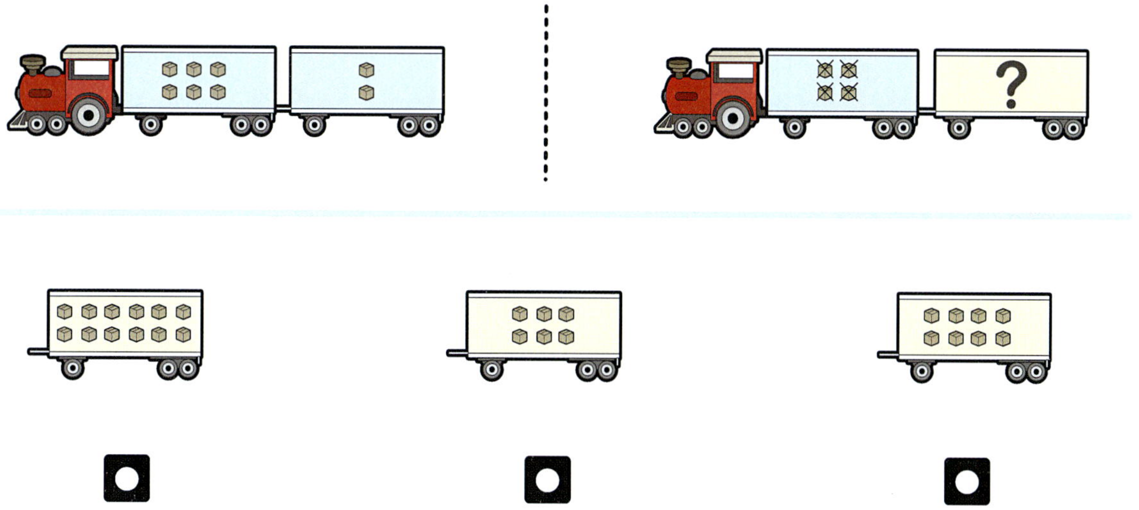

11

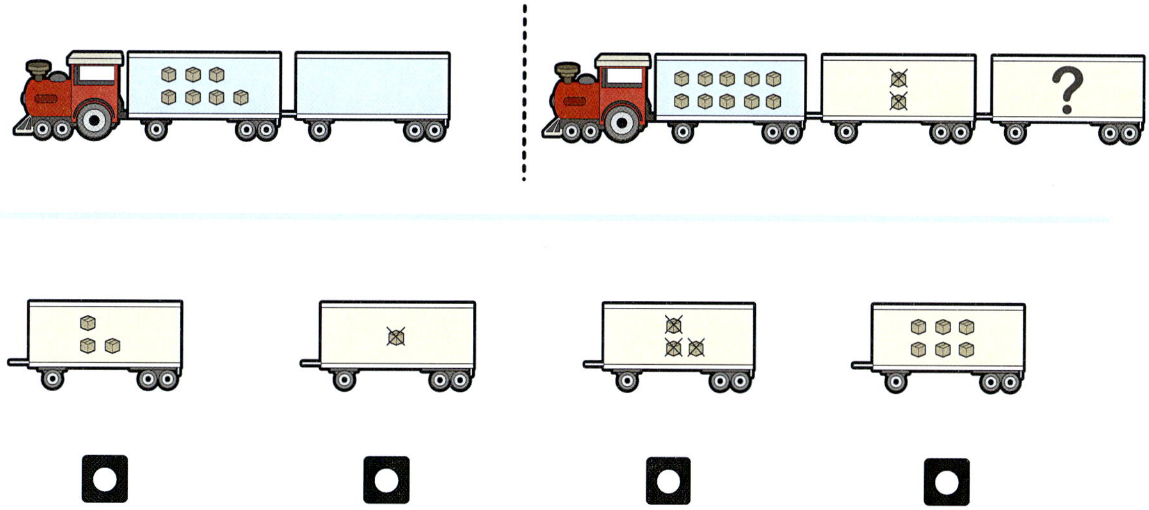

12

CogAT® Practice Test Level 7 - Questions   Bright Kids NYC Inc ©

Test Six:
Number Series

CogAT® **Practice Test Level 7 - Questions**   Bright Kids NYC Inc ©

S1

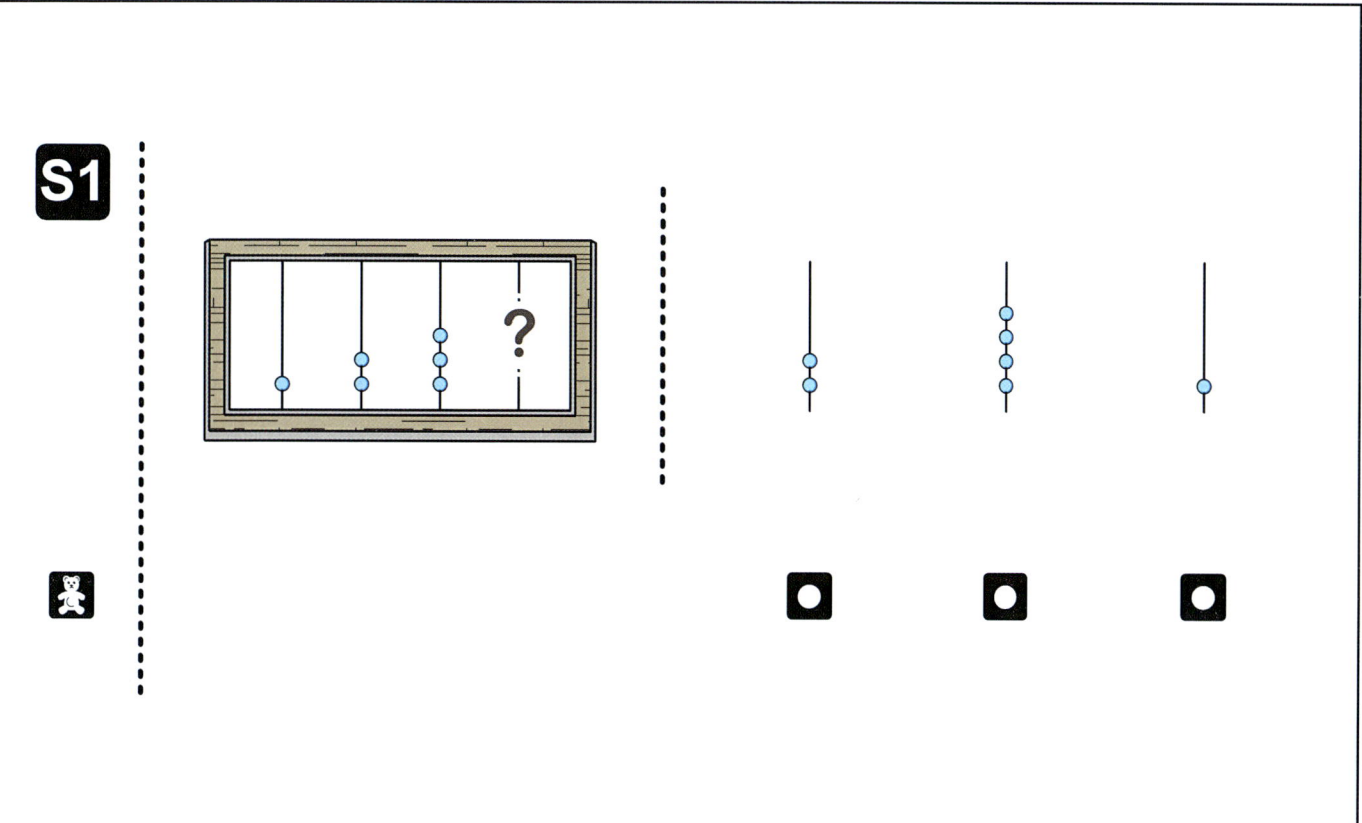

01

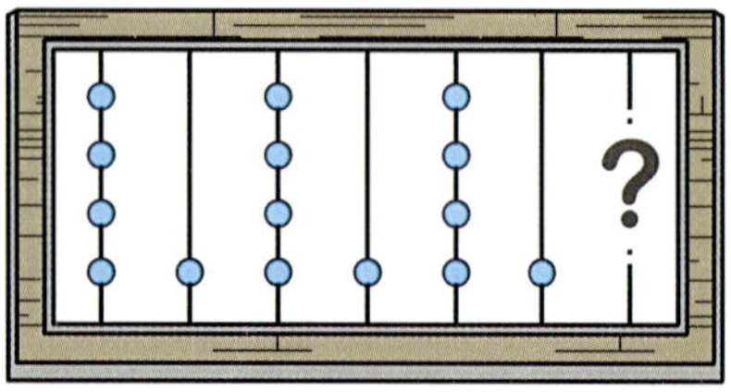

02

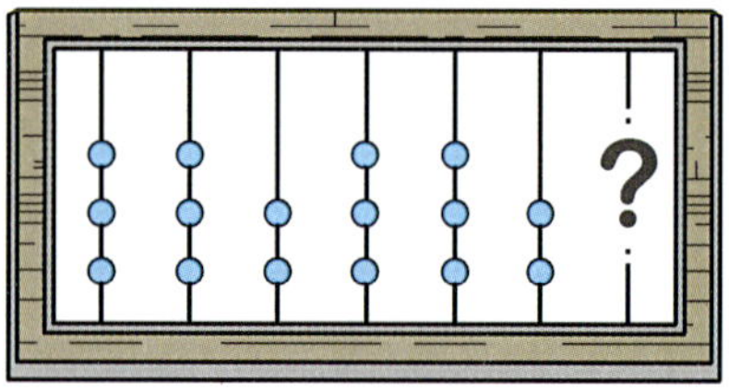

03

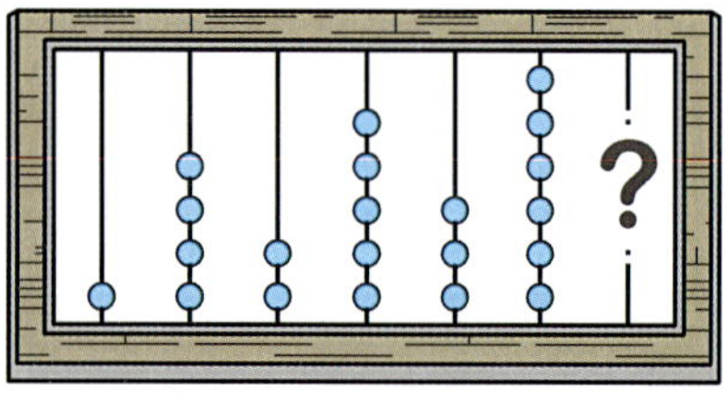

CogAT® Practice Test Level 7 - Questions   Bright Kids NYC Inc ©

04

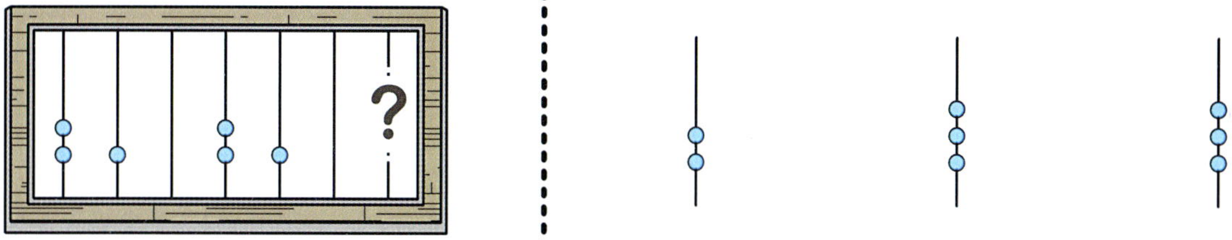

?

○   ○   ○

05

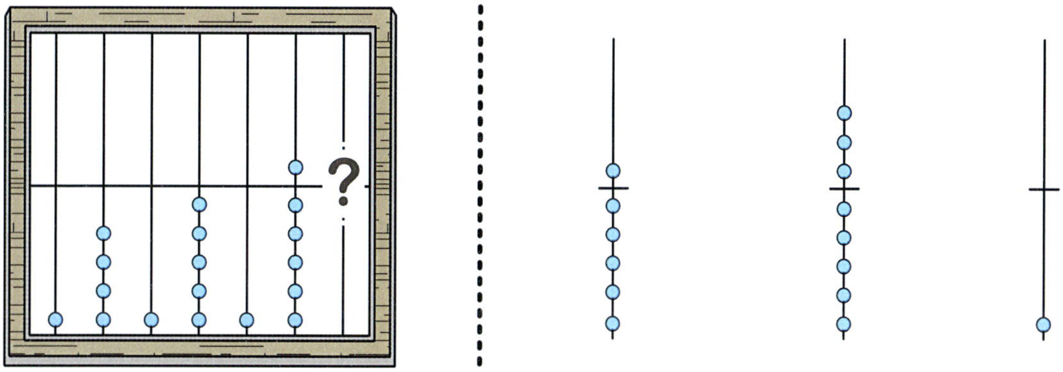

?

○   ○   ○

06

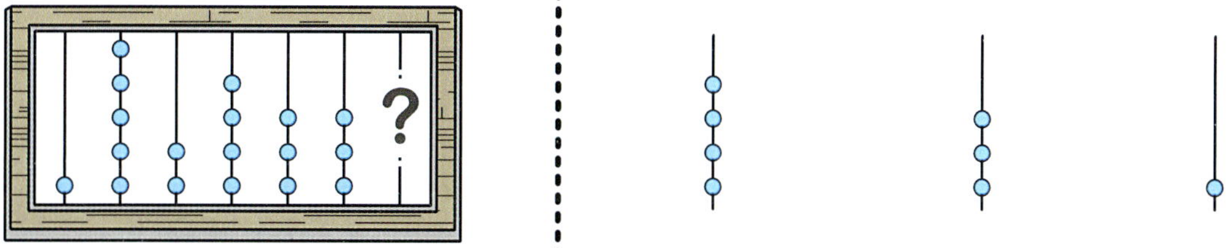

?

○   ○   ○

07

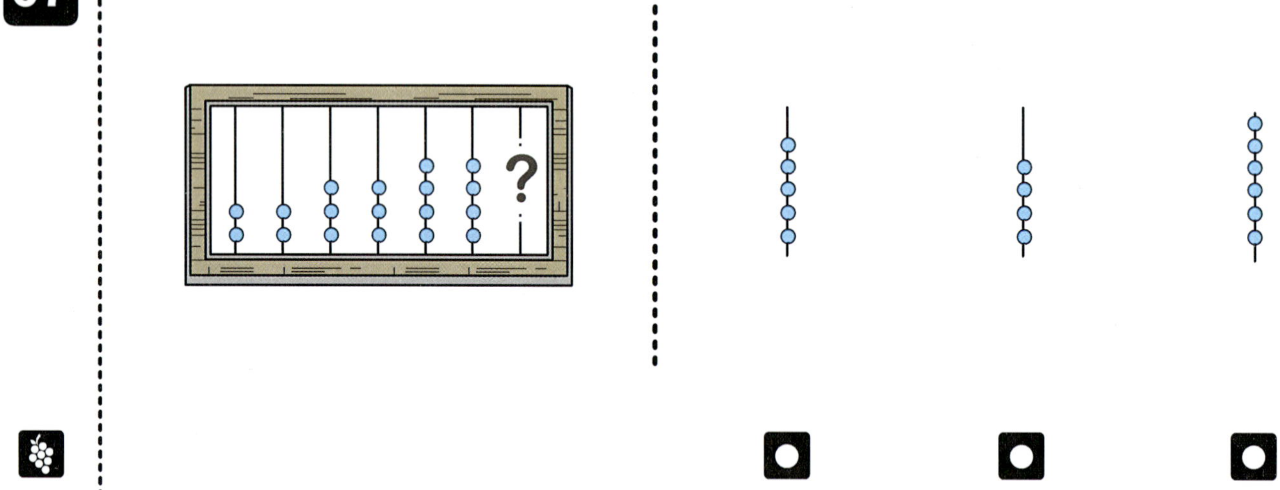

08

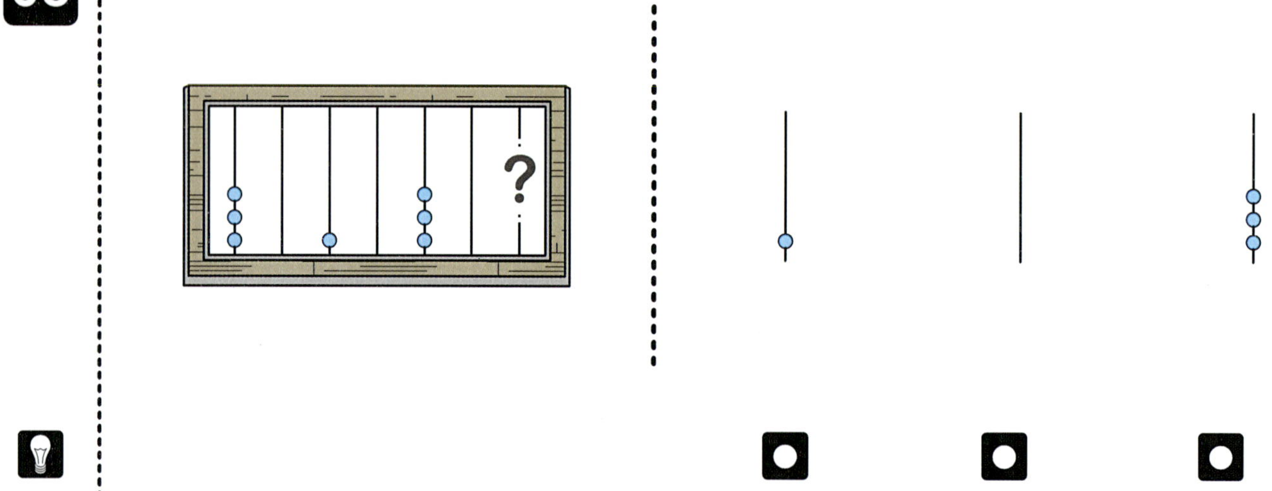

09

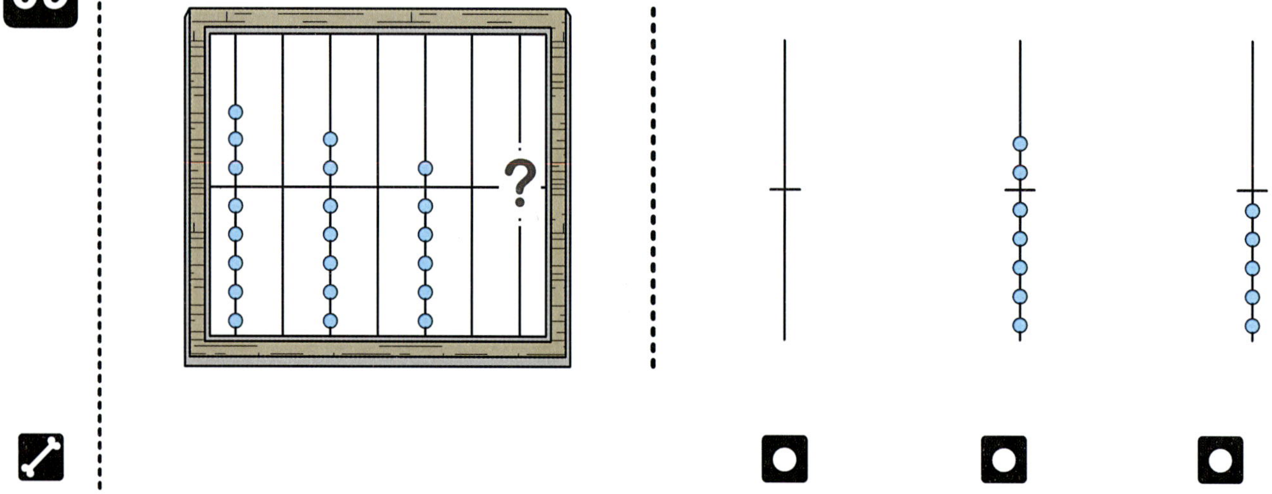

CogAT® Practice Test Level 7 - Questions   Bright Kids NYC Inc ©

10

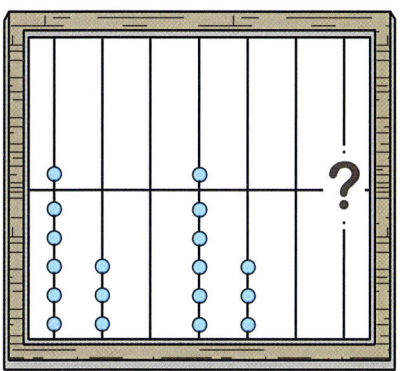

11

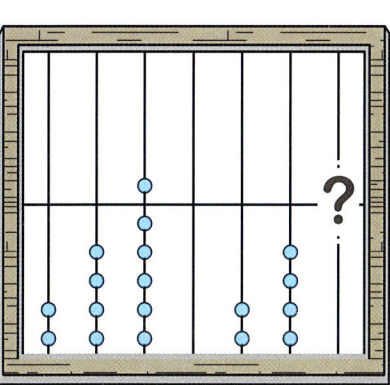

12

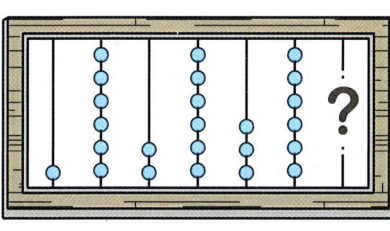

13

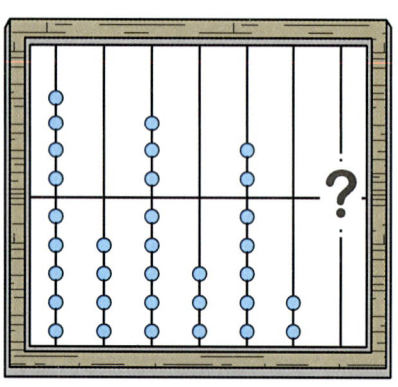

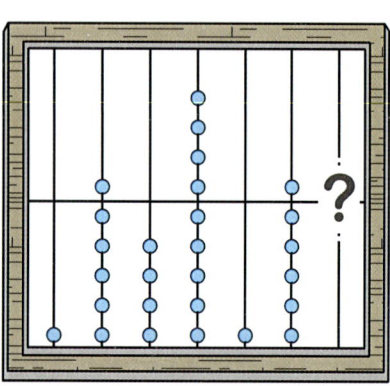

14

15

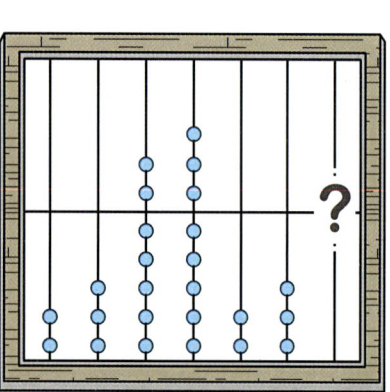

CogAT® Practice Test Level 7 - Questions   Bright Kids NYC Inc ©

16

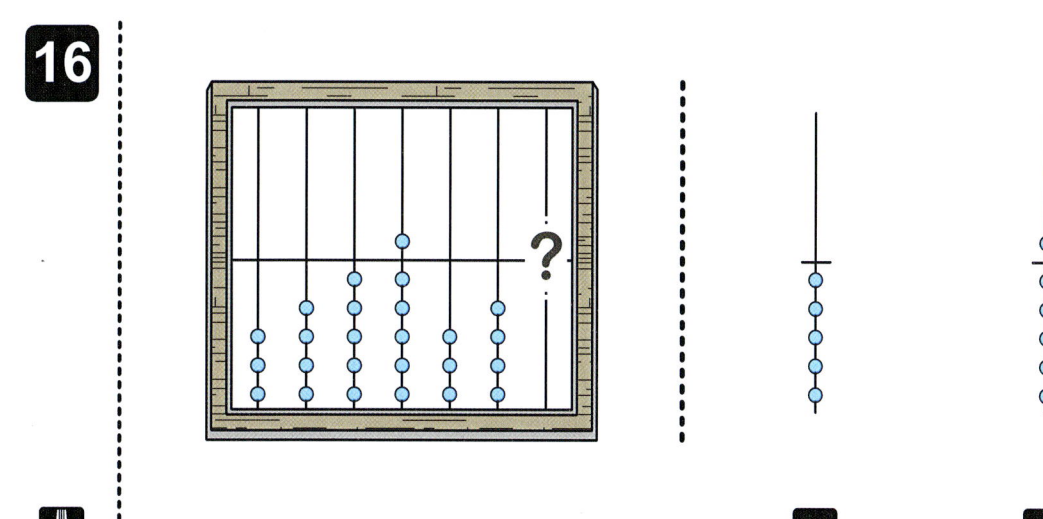

CogAT® Practice Test Level 7 - Questions   Bright Kids NYC Inc ©

Test Seven:
Figure Matrices

CogAT® **Practice Test Level 7 - Questions**   Bright Kids NYC Inc ©

S1

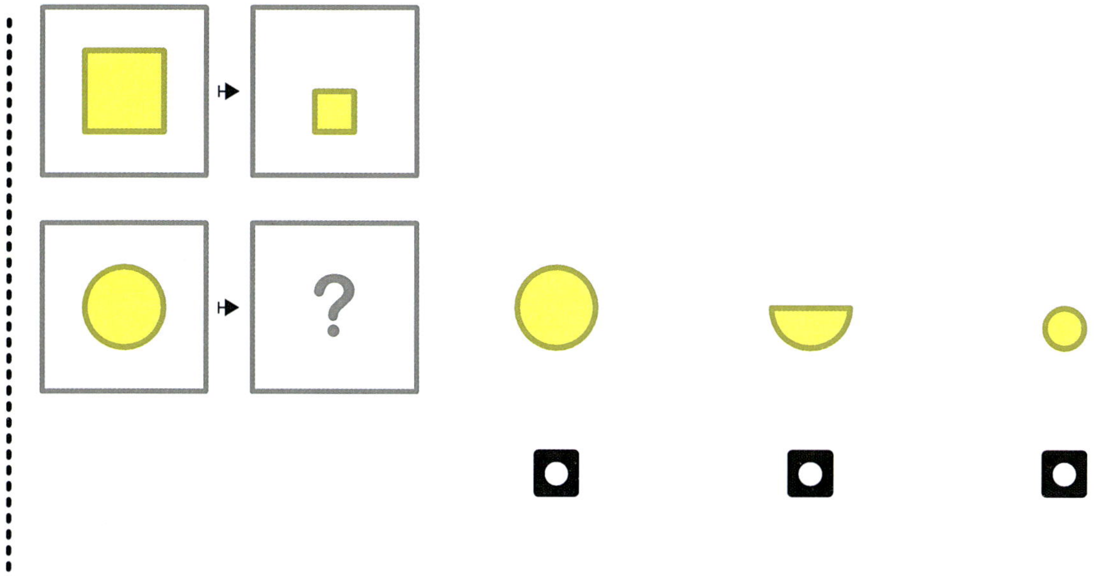

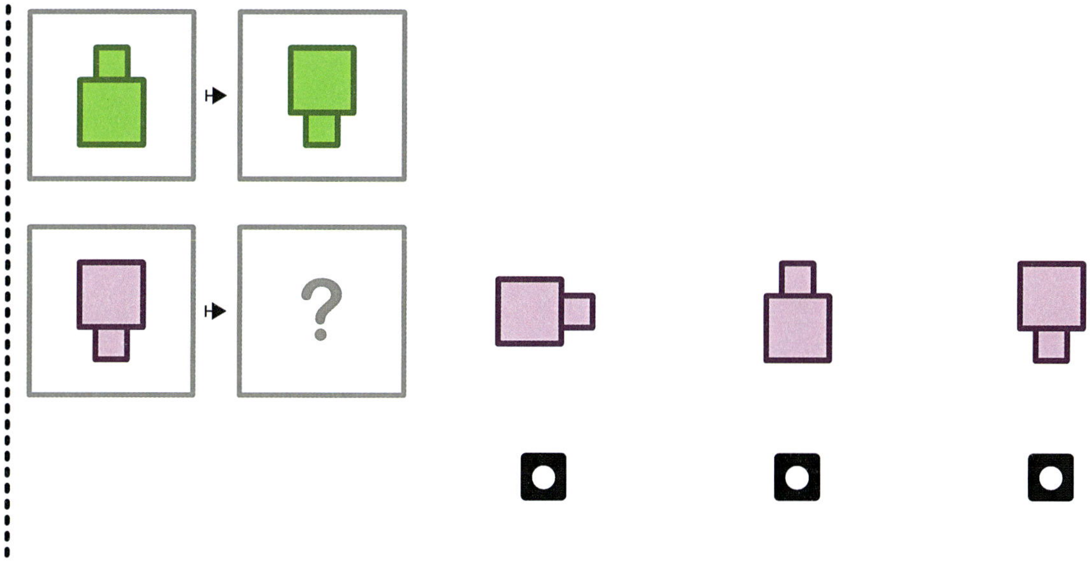

01

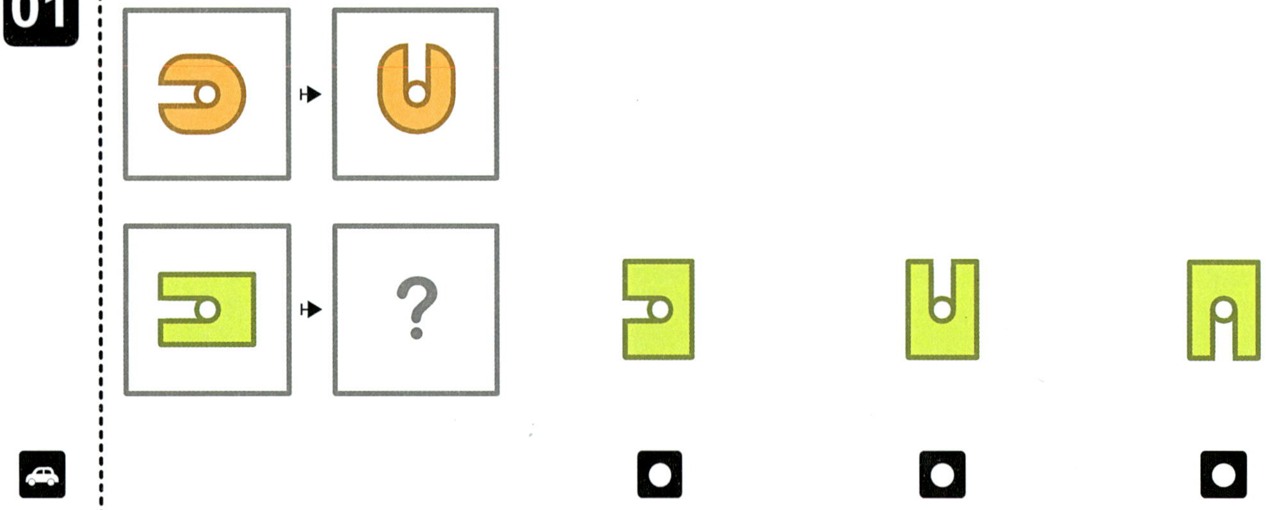

02

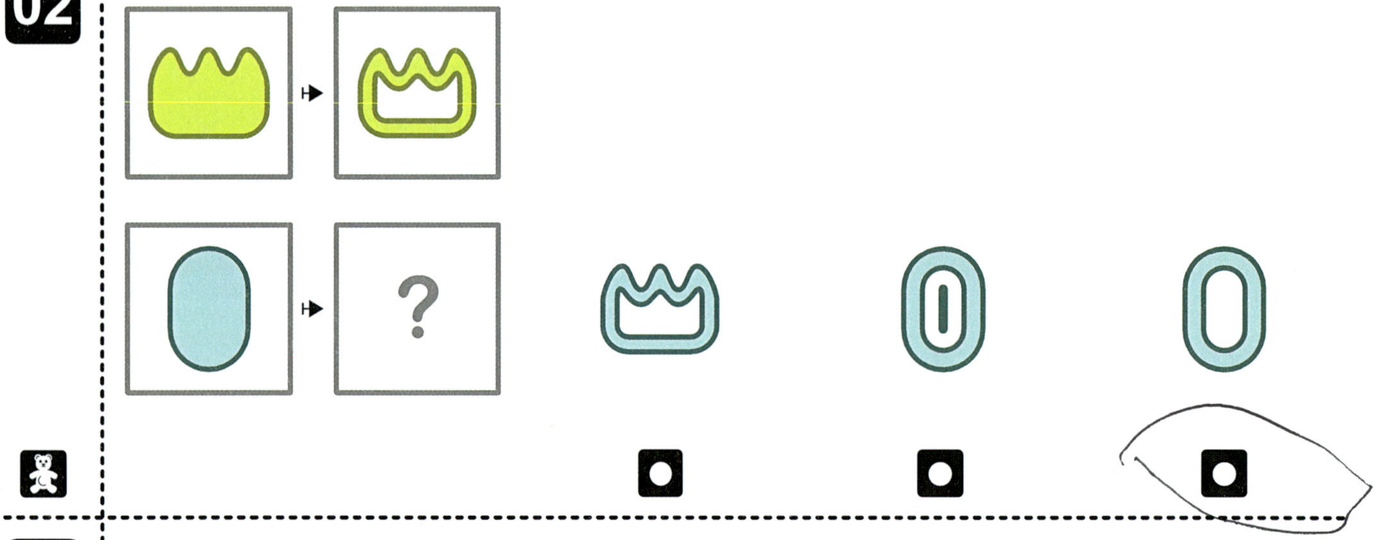

03

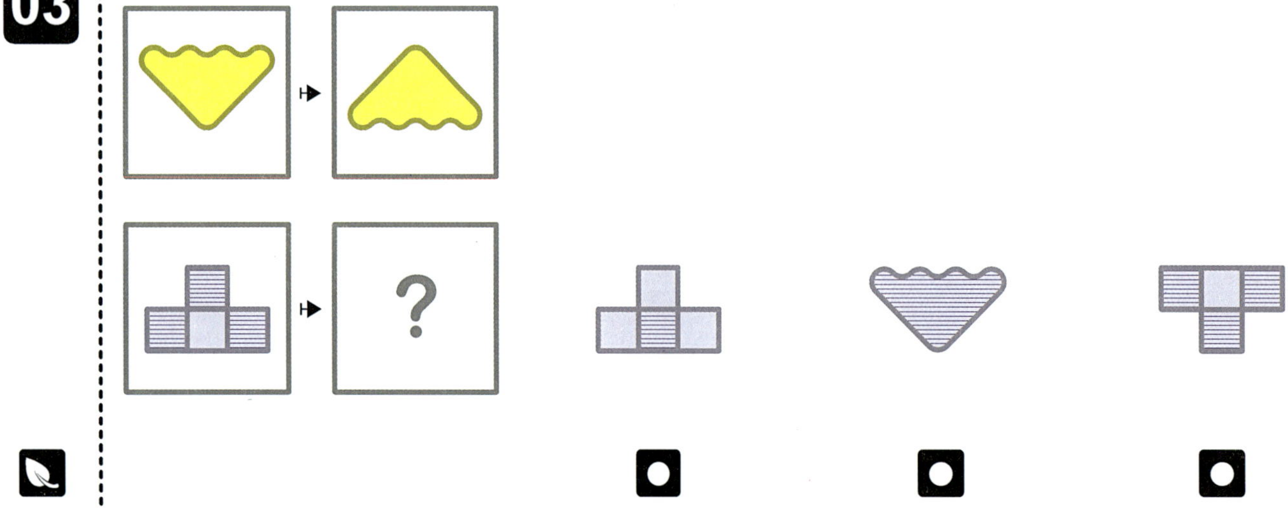

04

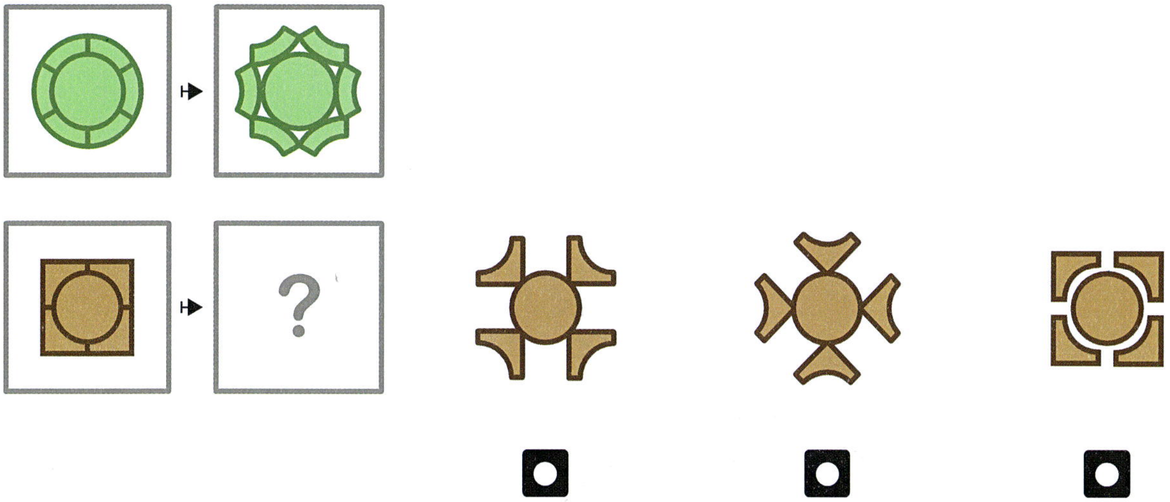

05

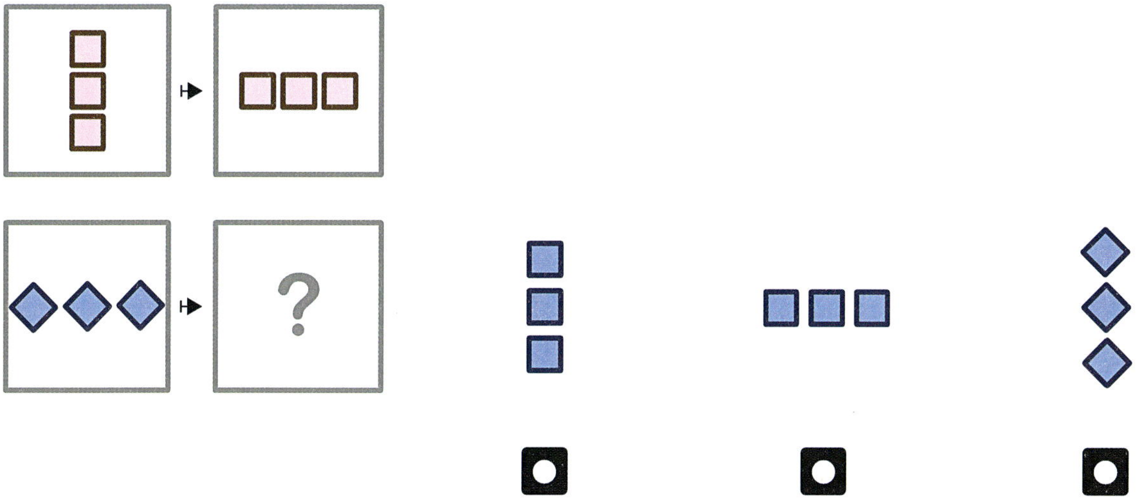

06

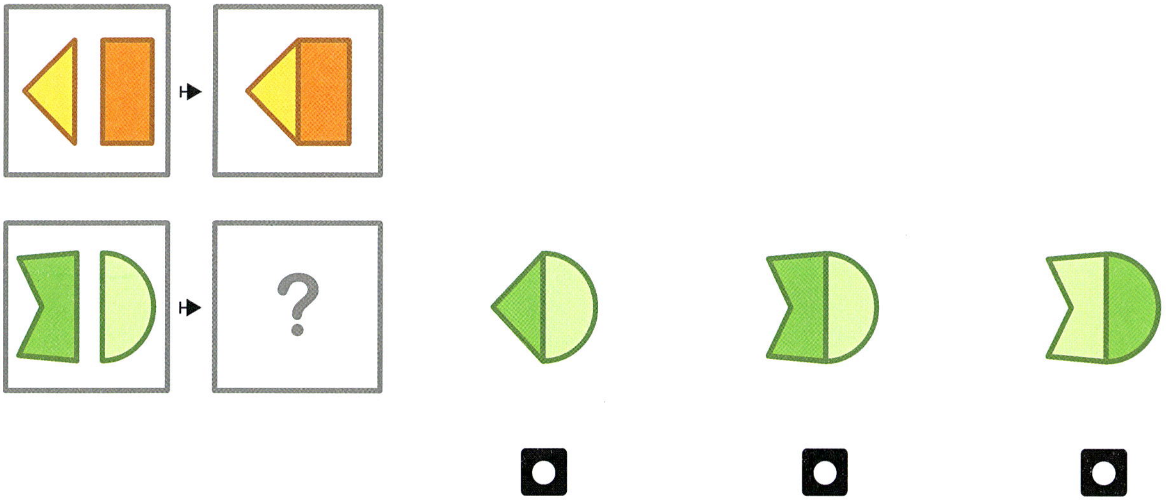

07

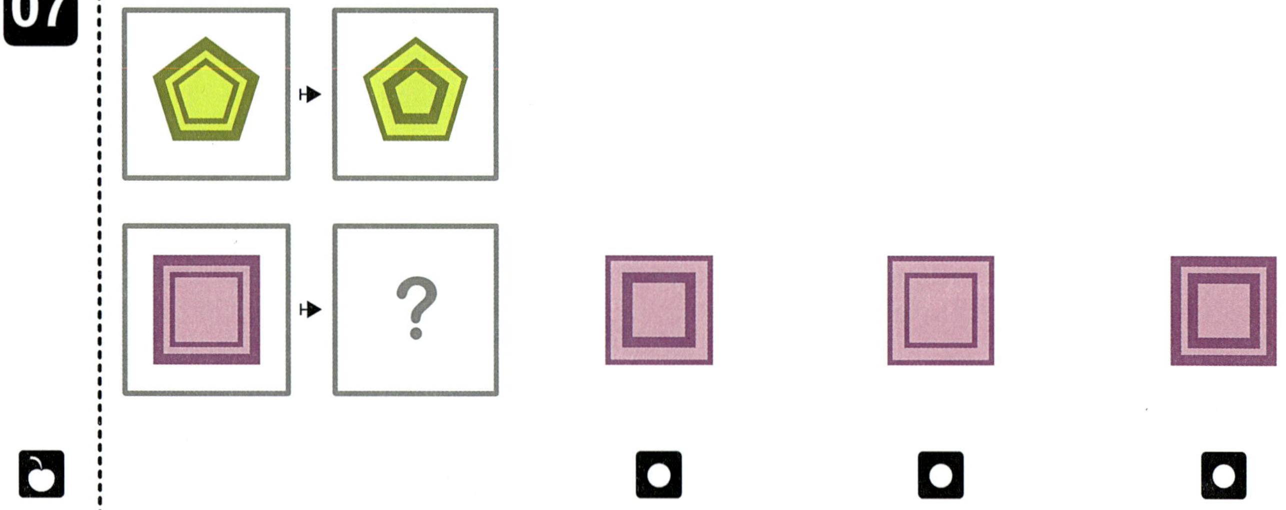

08

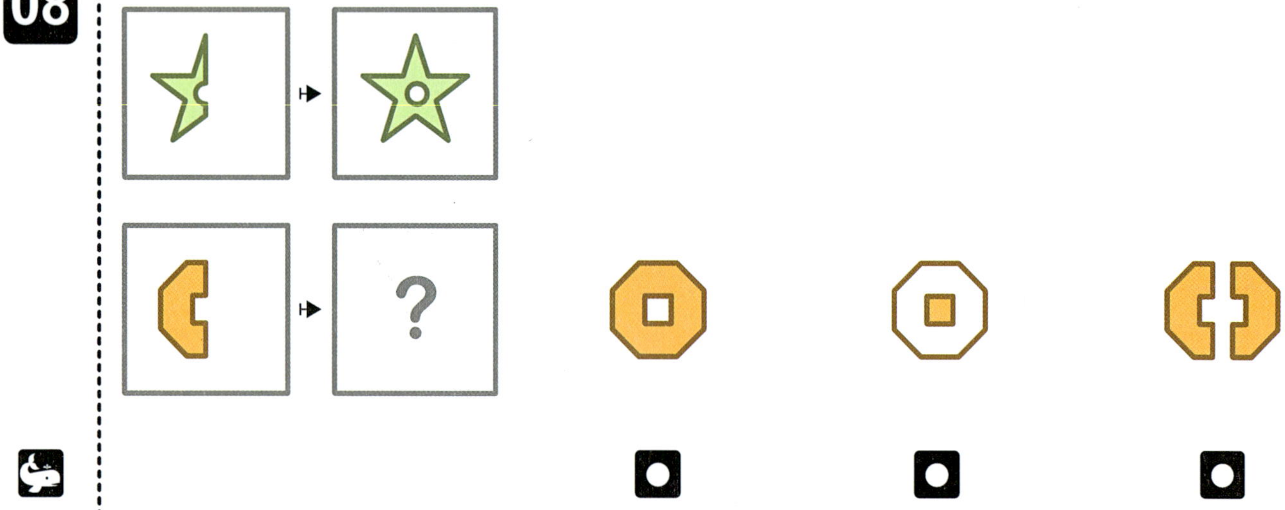

09

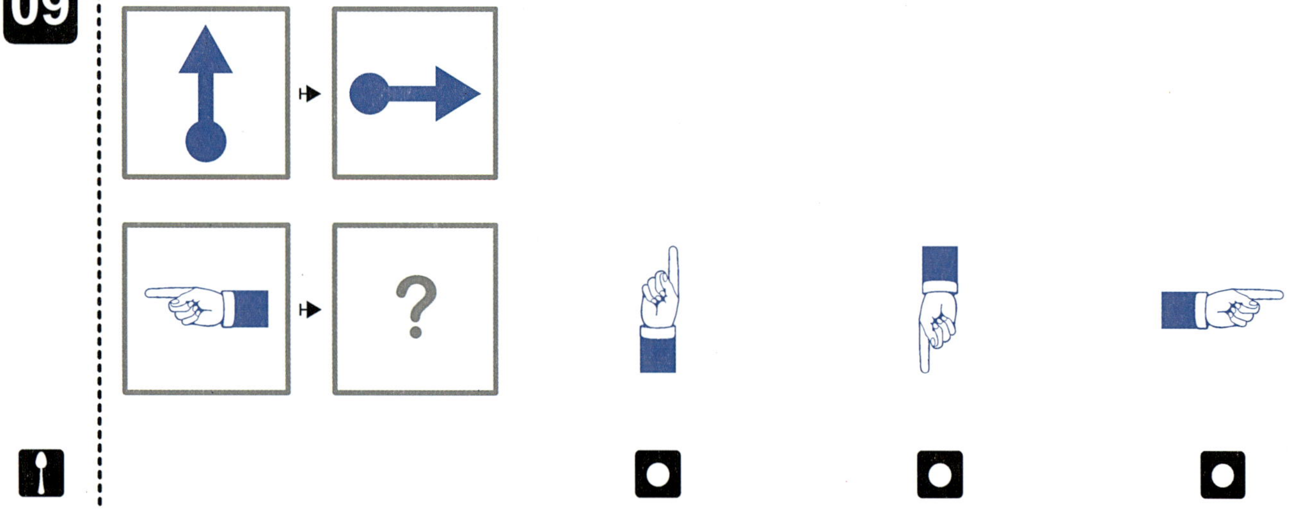

CogAT® Practice Test Level 7 - Questions   Bright Kids NYC Inc ©

10

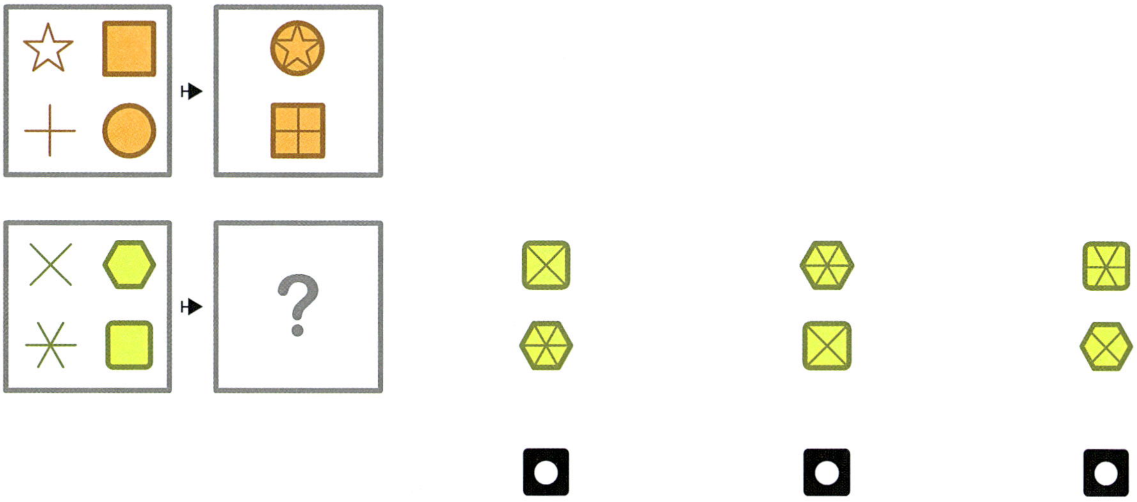

11

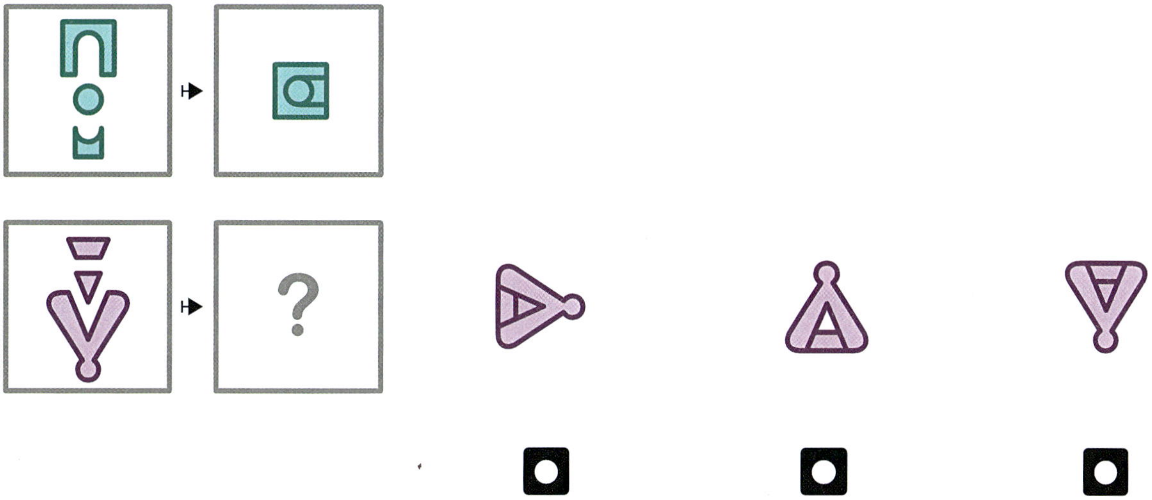

12

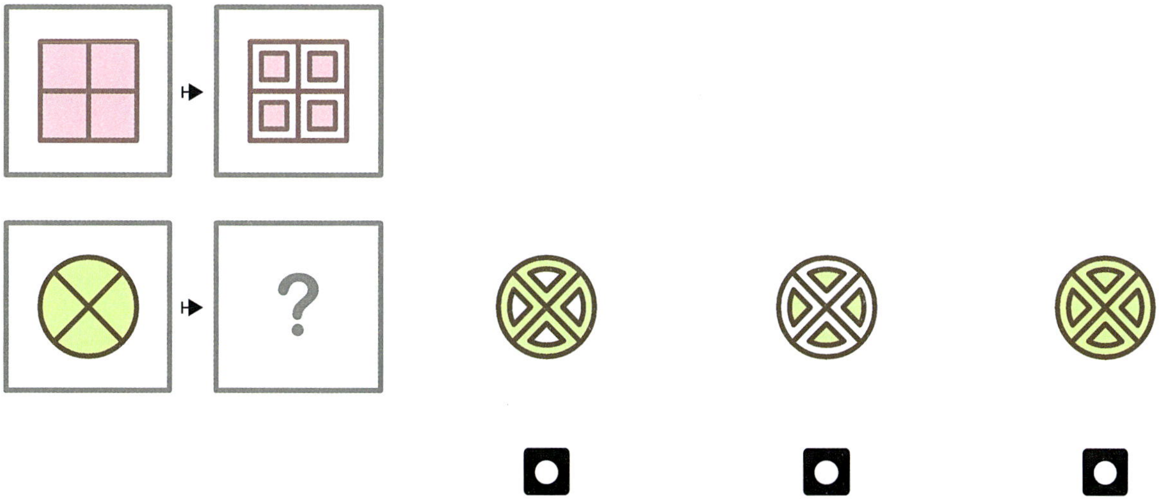

13

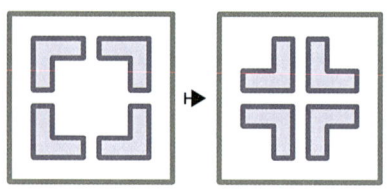

14

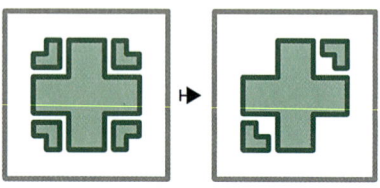

15

16

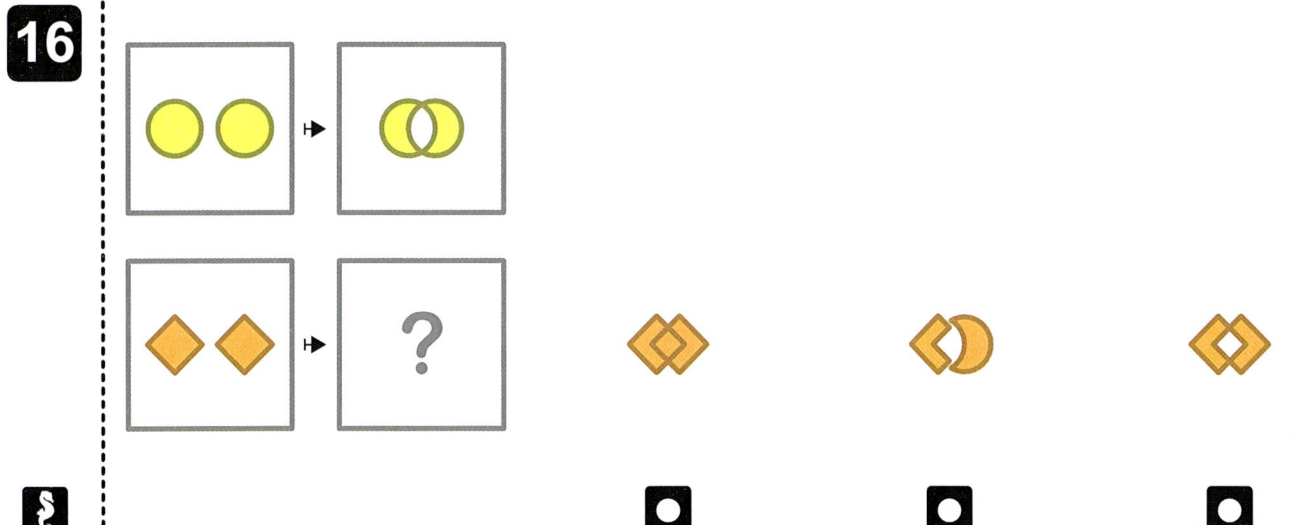

Test Eight:
Paper Folding

CogAT® Practice Test Level 7 - Questions

S1

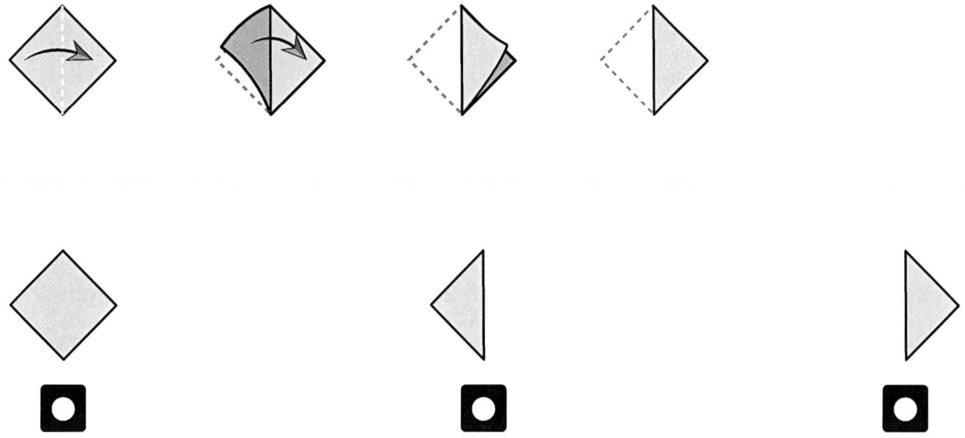

S2

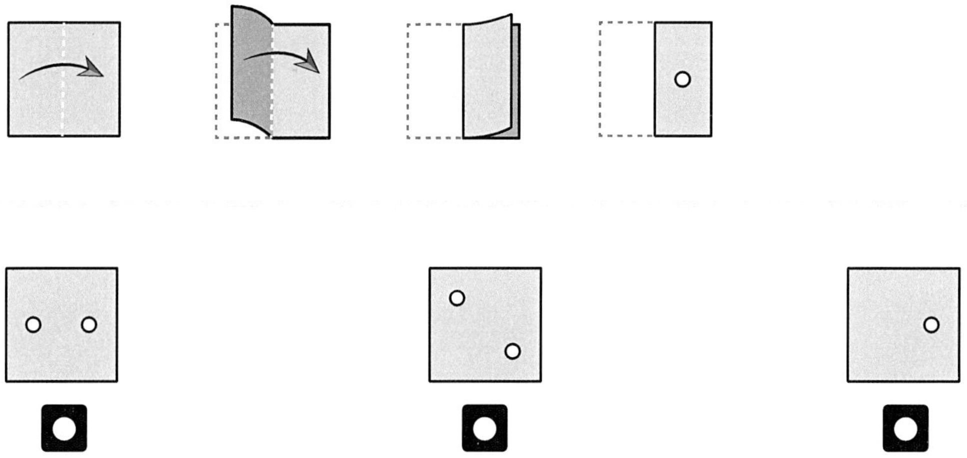

01

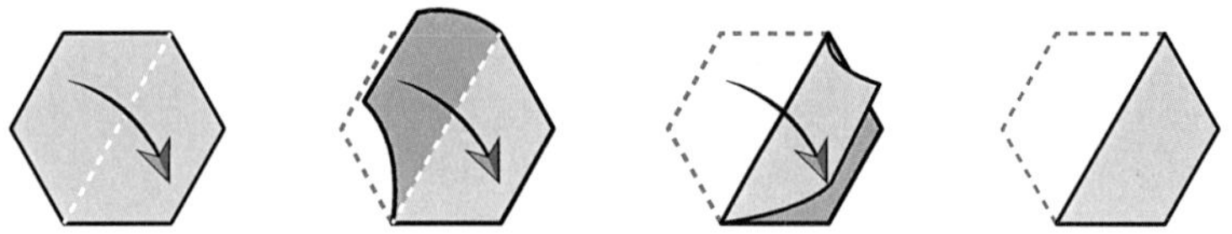

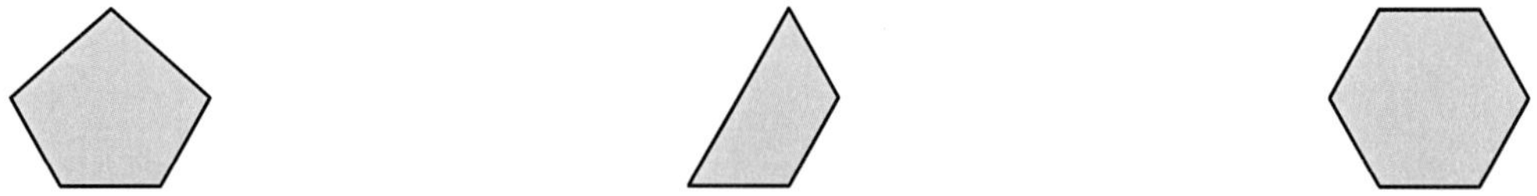

02

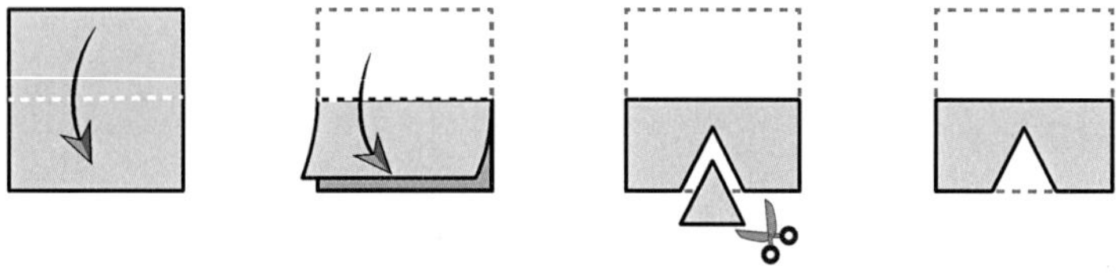

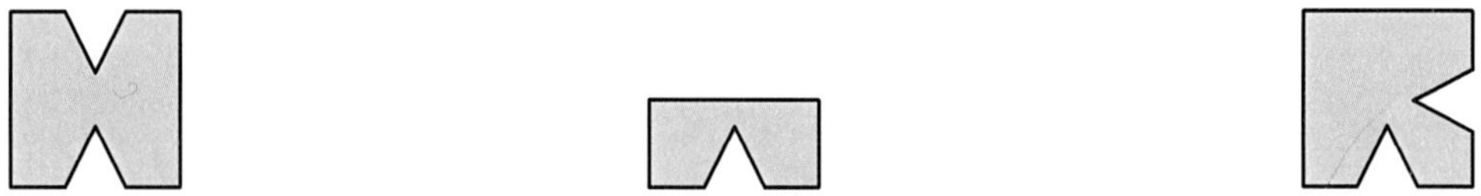

03

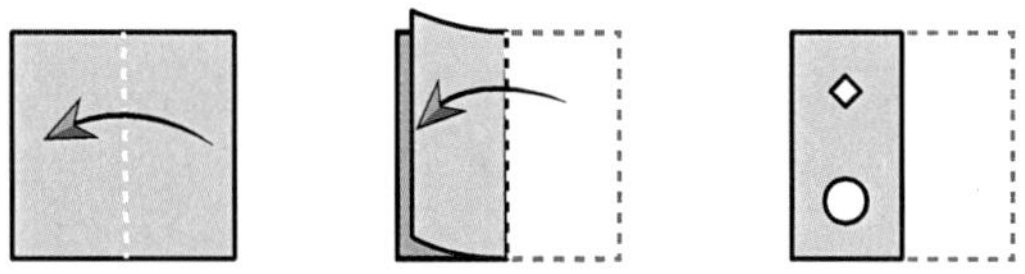

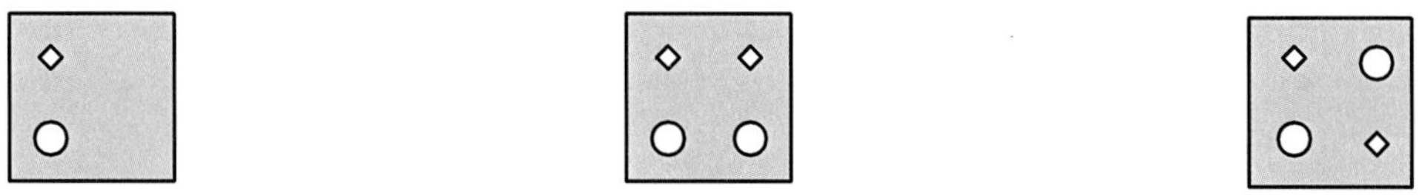

CogAT® Practice Test Level 7 - Questions Bright Kids NYC Inc ©

04

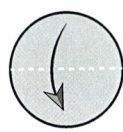 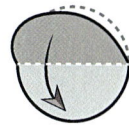  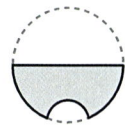

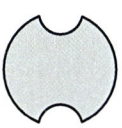  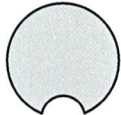

05

  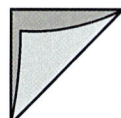 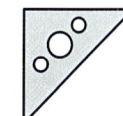

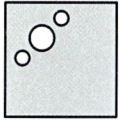 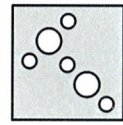 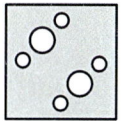

06

  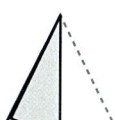 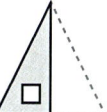

  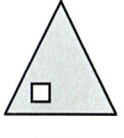

07

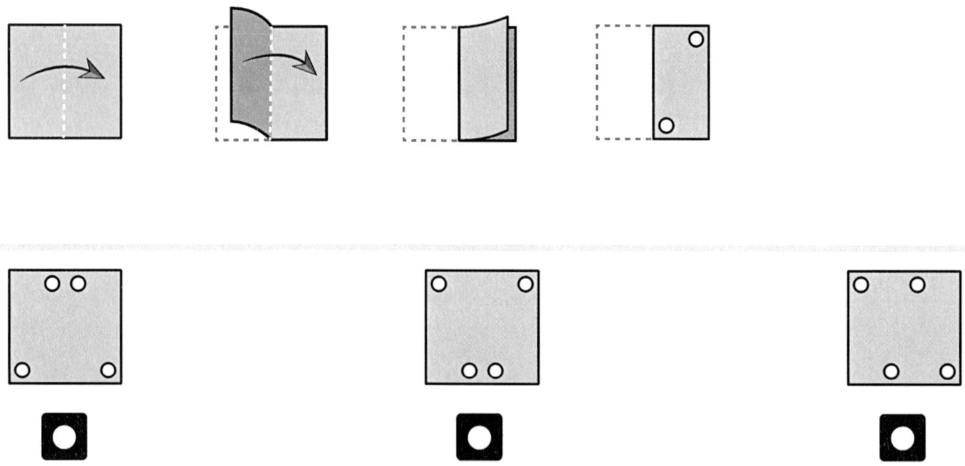

♡

08

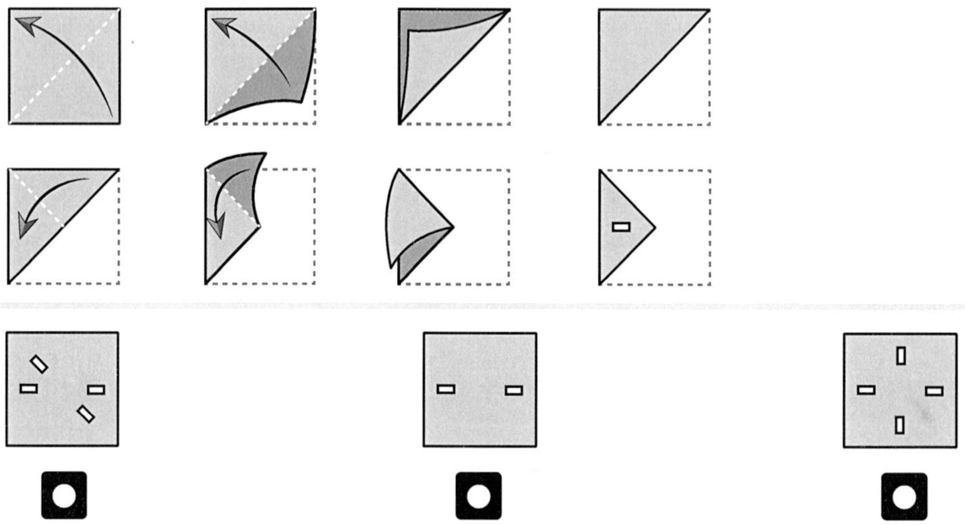

✏

09

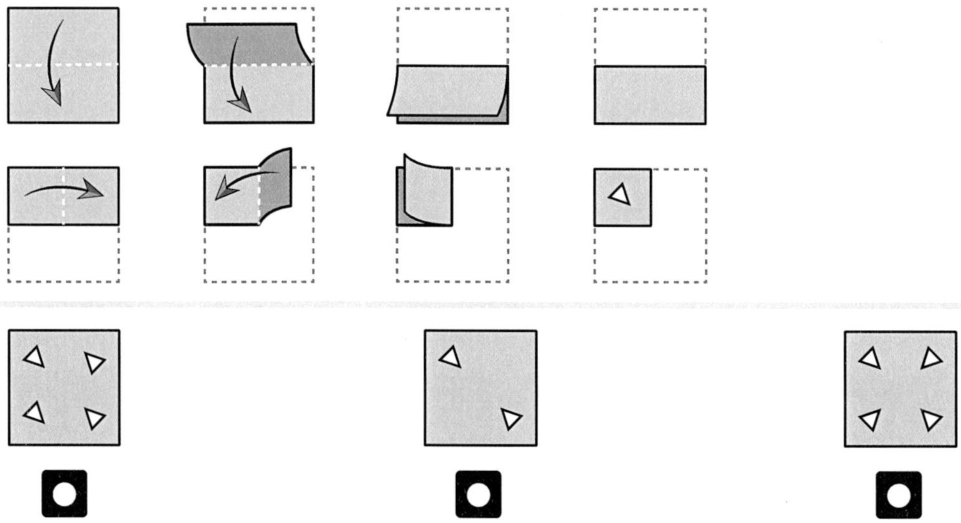

🪁

10

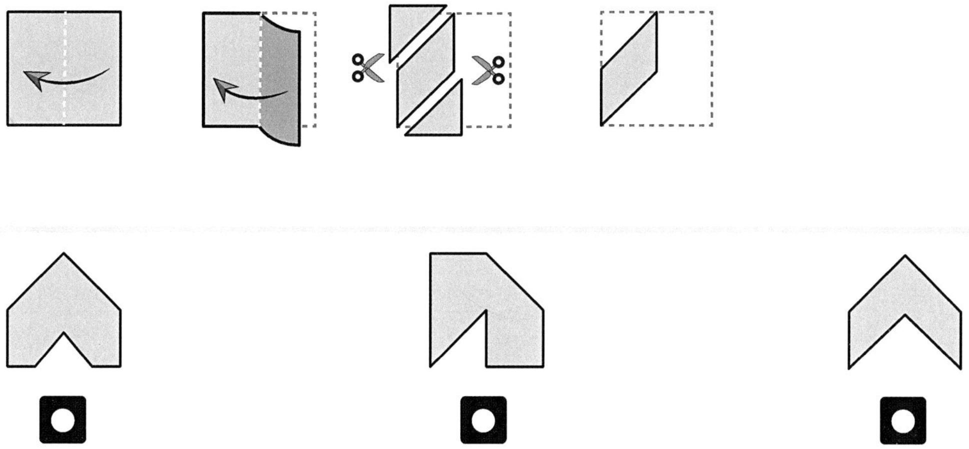

11

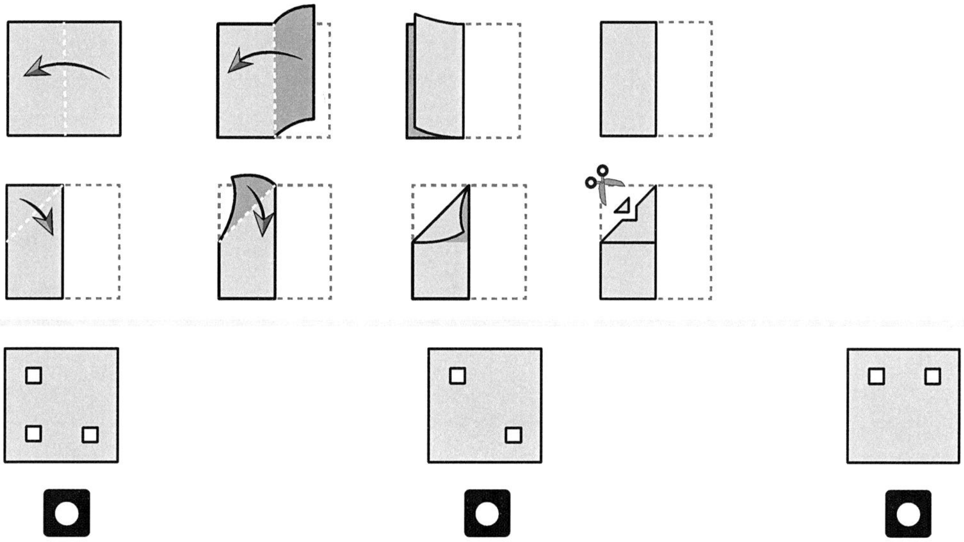

12

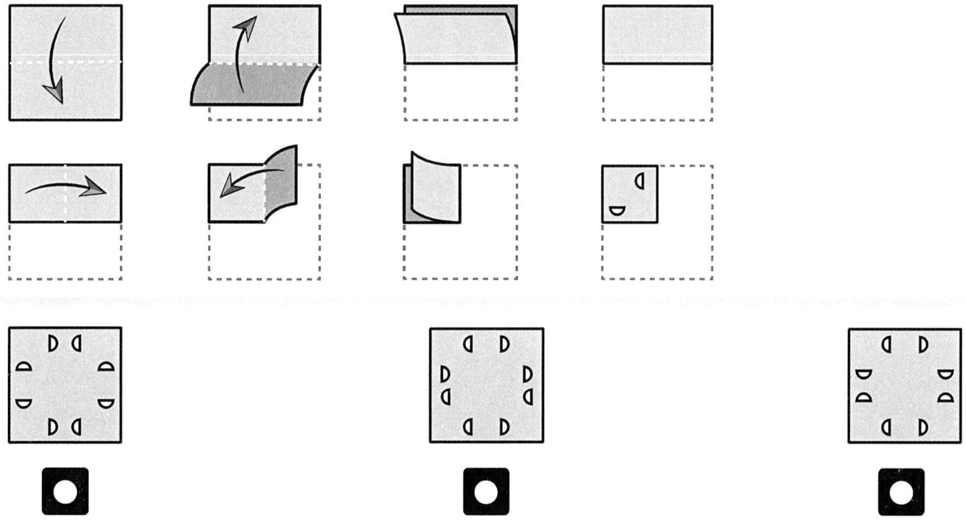

CogAT® **Practice Test Level 7 - Questions**

Test Nine:
Figure Classification

S1

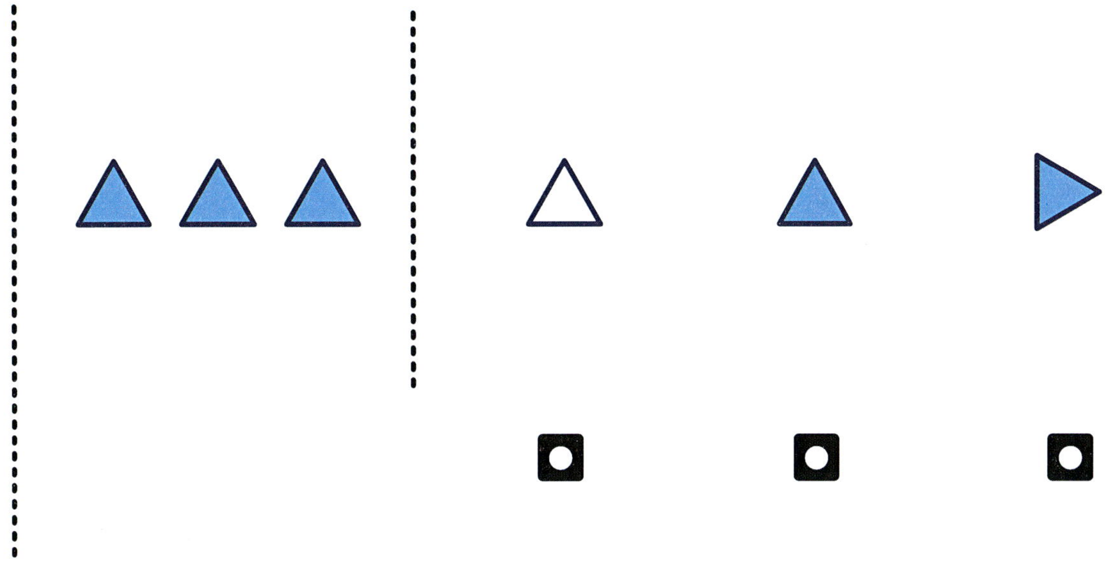

S2

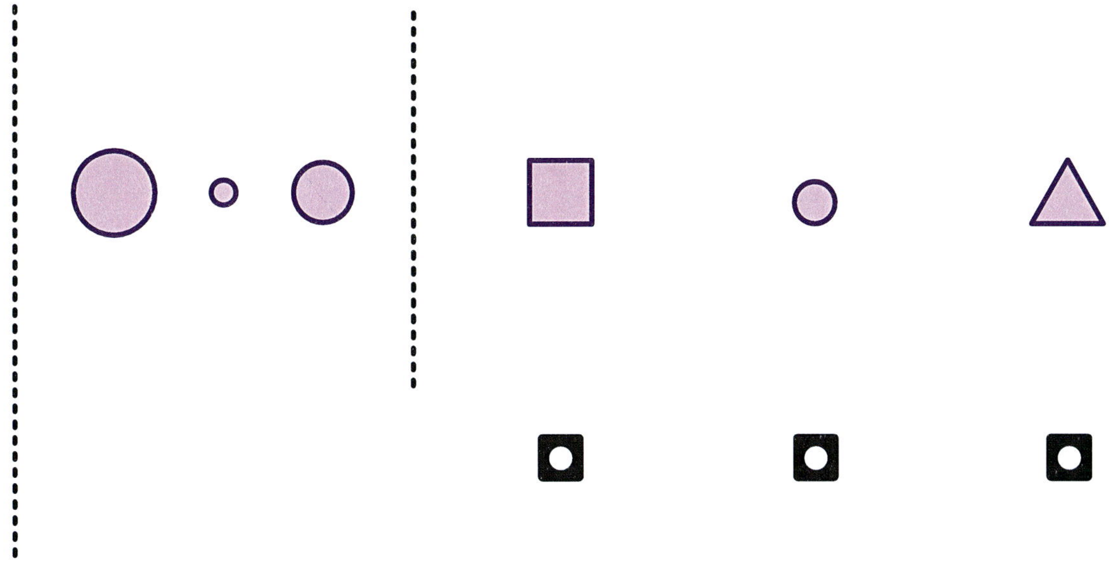

01

   |

02

   |

03

   |

CogAT® **Practice Test Level 7 - Questions** Bright Kids NYC Inc ©

04

   ○   ○   ○

05

○   ○   ○

06

  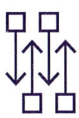   

○   ○   ○

07

08

09

CogAT® Practice Test Level 7 - Questions   Bright Kids NYC Inc ©

10

   |

11

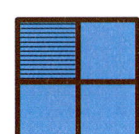 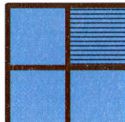  |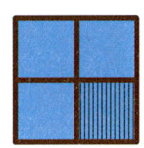

12

   |

13

14

15

CogAT® Practice Test Level 7 - Questions   Bright Kids NYC Inc ©

16